THE **100** MOST ASKED QUESTIONS ABOUT HEAVEN, HELL, AND THE AFTERLIFE

Books by S. Michael Houdmann

The 100 Most Asked Questions about God and the Bible

The 100 Most Asked Questions about Heaven, Hell, and the Afterlife

THE 100 MOST ASKED QUESTIONS ABOUT HEAVEN, HELL, AND THE AFTERLIFE

• • •

Scripture's Answers to
What Happens after You Die

S. Michael Houdmann

BETHANYHOUSE
a division of Baker Publishing Group
Minneapolis, Minnesota

Published by Bethany House Publishers
Minneapolis, Minnesota
BethanyHouse.com

Bethany House Publishers is a division of
Baker Publishing Group, Grand Rapids, Michigan

Printed in the United States of America

Library of Congress Cataloging-in-Publication Data
Names: Houdmann, S. Michael editor
Title: The 100 most asked questions about heaven, hell, and the afterlife : scripture's answers to what happens after you die / S. Michael Houdmann.
Other titles: Hundred most asked questions about heaven, hell, and the afterlife | GotQuestions.org.
Description: Minneapolis, Minnesota : Bethany House, a division of Baker Publishing Group, [2025]
Identifiers: LCCN 2025016496 | ISBN 9780764245794 paperback | ISBN 9780764245985 casebound | ISBN 9781493452392 ebook
Subjects: LCSH: Heaven--Christianity | Hell—Christianity | Death—Religious aspects—Christianity | Future life—Christianity
Classification: LCC BT846.3 .A275 2025 | DDC 236/.2—dc23/eng/20250602
LC record available at https://lccn.loc.gov/2025016496

25 26 27 28 29 30 31   7 6 5 4 3 2 1

Contents

SECTION 3
Questions about the Afterlife   51

SECTION 4
General Questions about Heaven 73

SECTION 5
Questions about What Heaven Will Be Like 89

SECTION 8
Questions about What Hell Will Be Like 149

SECTION 9
Questions about Judgment and Eternity 167

SECTION 10

Questions about Alternate Afterlife Beliefs   187

Introduction

Little did I know what God had in mind when I launched Got Questions.org over twenty-two years ago. What my wife and I thought would be a fun hobby turned out to be something God intended to expand into one of the most impactful Christian websites in the world. Now, not only do I have my dream job, but I also get to watch God take our limited vision and use it in ways far beyond anything we could ask or imagine.

GotQuestions.org has received over one million personally submitted questions from around the world. Each month, the articles on GotQuestions.org are read approximately twenty million times. Over the years, our articles have been read over 2.5 billion times. These interactions give GotQuestions.org plenty of data regarding what questions people are truly asking. We *know* what people are asking. We *know* the information people are searching for. And, after years of God refining us and the content we produce, we have improved at answering questions in an understandable and applicable way.

This book contains the top one hundred questions we have received related to heaven, hell, eternity, and the afterlife. Many of the questions are of vital importance. Some of the questions are immensely personal. A few of the questions are fairly obscure. None of the questions are trivial.

My sincerest hope is that you will find this resource interesting, informative, biblically accurate, and worth sharing with others. My utmost desire would be that you would come to an understanding of what God's Word says about eternity: how to get to heaven, how to avoid hell, what the afterlife will be like, and how to live your life in the here and now in light of the world to come. May this book motivate you to continue asking questions and continue looking to God's Word for the answers.

—S. Michael Houdmann

SECTION 1
Questions about Salvation

1. What is eternal life?

When the Bible speaks of eternal life, it refers to a gift of God that comes only "in Christ Jesus our Lord" (Romans 6:23). This gift contrasts with the natural result of sin: "death."

The gift of eternal life comes to those who believe in Jesus Christ, who is Himself "the resurrection and the life" (John 11:25). The fact that this life is eternal indicates that it is *perpetual* life—it goes on and on and on, with no end.

It is a mistake, however, to view eternal life as simply an unending progression of years. A common New Testament word for "eternal" is *aiónios*, which carries the idea of *quality* as well as *quantity*. In fact, eternal life is not really associated with years at all, as it is independent of time. Eternal life can function outside of and beyond time, as well as within time.

For this reason, eternal life can be thought of as something that Christians experience *now*. Believers don't have to wait for eternal life, because it's not something that starts when they die. Rather, eternal life begins the moment a person exercises faith in Christ. It is our current possession. John 3:36 says, "Whoever believes in the Son has eternal life." Note that the believer "has" (present tense) this life (the verb is present tense in the Greek, too). We find similar present-tense constructions in John 5:24 and John 6:47. The focus of eternal life is not on our future but on our current standing in Christ.

The Bible inextricably links eternal life with the person of Jesus Christ. John 17:3 is an important passage in this regard, as Jesus prays, "Now this is eternal life: that they know you, the only true God, and Jesus Christ, whom you have sent." Here, Jesus equates eternal life with a knowledge of God and of the Son. There is no knowledge of God without the Son, for it is through the Son that the Father reveals Himself to the elect (John 17:6; 14:9).

This life-giving knowledge of the Father and the Son is a true, personal knowledge, not just an academic awareness. There will be some on Judgment Day who had claimed to be followers of Christ but never really had a relationship with Him. To those pretenders, Jesus will say, "I never knew you. Away from me, you evildoers!" (Matthew 7:23). The apostle Paul made it his goal to *know* the Lord, and he linked that knowledge to the resurrection from the dead: "I want to know Christ—yes, to know the power of his resurrection and participation in his sufferings, becoming like him in his death, and so, somehow, attaining to the resurrection from the dead" (Philippians 3:10–11).

In the New Jerusalem, the apostle John sees a river "flowing from the throne of God and of the Lamb. . . . On each side of the river stood the tree of life. . . . And the leaves of the tree are for the healing of the nations" (Revelation 22:1–2). In Eden, we rebelled against God and were banished from the tree of life (Genesis 3:24). In the end, God graciously restores our access to the tree of life.

This access is provided through Jesus Christ, "the Lamb of God, who takes away the sin of the world" (John 1:29).

Right now, every sinner is invited to know Christ and to receive eternal life: "Let the one who is thirsty come; and let the one who wishes take the free gift of the water of life" (Revelation 22:17).

How can you know that you have eternal life? First, confess your sin before God. Then accept God's provision of a Savior on your behalf. Jesus Christ, the Son of God, died for your sins, and He rose again the third day. Believe this good news; trust the Lord Jesus as your Savior, and you will be saved (Acts 16:31; Romans 10:9–10). "Everyone who calls on the name of the Lord will be saved" (Romans 10:13).

John puts it so simply: "God has given us eternal life, and this life is in his Son. Whoever has the Son has life; whoever does not have the Son of God does not have life" (1 John 5:11–12).

2. What determines if a person goes to heaven or hell?

John 3:16–18 says, "For God so loved the world that he gave his one and only Son, that whoever believes in him shall not perish but have eternal life. For God did not send his Son into the world to condemn the world, but to save the world through him. Whoever believes in him is not condemned, but whoever does not believe stands condemned already because they have not believed in the name of God's one and only Son." Apart from the work of Jesus Christ, every human is condemned to an eternity in hell (Revelation 20:15). But God has freely offered the gift of heaven. What determines if a person goes to heaven or hell for eternity is whether that person has been reconciled to God through Jesus Christ (Romans 4; Galatians 3:23–29; Hebrews 11).

Going to hell is the default position of humanity. Going to heaven is the free gift of God's grace, received by faith, offered to all people (Ephesians 2:1–10). God wants people to be reconciled with Him, so He provided the way (John 14:6). Every person is invited to go to heaven.

Going to heaven or hell has everything to do with God's act of rescue. When God created the world, everything was very good (Genesis 1:31). He created humanity in His image. He provided food for them but told them there was one tree from which they were not allowed to eat. They were to trust His provision, follow His commands, remain in close relationship with Him, and experience fullness of life. But they were also free to disobey Him, which would result in death (Genesis 2:15–17; Romans 6:23).

Adam and Eve, the first humans, ate the forbidden fruit (Genesis 3). This act of rebellion is commonly called "original sin," and it has lasting effects. Our relationships with God, with one another, and with the created world are broken. Death is now a reality in our world. The sin of Adam is passed down to all his descendants—all of humanity (Romans 5:12).

But even as God explained to Adam and Eve what their disobedience would mean, He promised a Savior (Genesis 3:15, 21)! One would come who would ultimately restore humanity to God.

That Savior is Jesus Christ. Jesus is "God with us" (Matthew 1:20–23). He is fully God and fully human. He was conceived of the Holy Spirit and born to a virgin named Mary. He is God in the flesh, the one who reconciles humans and God (1 John 4:2). He is the Creator who entered into His creation in order to restore it to Himself (Colossians 1:15–19).

Jesus lived a fully human life—He was tempted to sin as we are—but He perfectly obeyed all of God's ways (Romans 5:12–21; Hebrews 4:14–16). He willingly died on the cross as a payment for our sin (John 10:17–18; Hebrews 9:14–10:18; 1 Peter 3:18). From the cross, He proclaimed, "It is finished" (John 19:30). Jesus rose from the dead, demonstrating that He is who He claims and that He is victorious over sin and death (1 Corinthians 15:3–8, 50–57). All who put their faith in Him receive forgiveness of sin

(Colossians 2:13–15). Jesus takes their sin and gives them His righteousness (2 Corinthians 5:18–21; Ephesians 2:1–10). Because of that forgiveness, they will go to heaven.

Whether a person goes to heaven or hell has everything to do with their response to God. He freely offers the gift of eternity in heaven with Him. He invites everyone to believe, to receive His rescue, and to enjoy fullness of life in Him (Hebrews 4:1–13).

Do you know whether you will go to heaven or hell? If not, settle the issue now. If you have questions about who God is or what salvation is, please visit us at www.gotquestions.org. If you understand that you are separated from God and that He has provided the means of forgiveness and reconciliation, receive His offer of salvation by faith today! Romans 10:9–10 says, "If you declare with your mouth, 'Jesus is Lord,' and believe in your heart that God raised him from the dead, you will be saved. For it is with your heart that you believe and are justified, and it is with your mouth that you profess your faith and are saved."

3. Where did Old Testament believers/saints go when they died?

People living in the times of the Old Testament were saved in the same way we are: by God's grace through faith. Salvation came through faith in the promise of the Messiah (Isaiah 53:5–6). Old Testament believers went to a place of comfort and rest called paradise when they died. The Old Testament taught life after death (Job 19:25–27) and that everyone who departed from this life went to a place of conscious existence. The general term for this place was *Sheol*, which could be translated "the grave" or "the realm of the dead." The wicked were there (Psalm 9:17; 31:17; 49:14; Isaiah 5:14), and so were the righteous (Genesis 37:35; Job 14:13; Psalm 6:5; 16:10; 88:3; Isaiah 38:10).

The New Testament equivalent of Sheol is Hades. Luke 16:19–31 shows that, prior to Christ's resurrection, Hades was divided into two realms: a place of comfort where Lazarus was (Abraham's bosom or Abraham's side) and a place of torment where the rich man was (hell). Lazarus's place of comfort is elsewhere called "paradise" (Luke 23:43). The place of torment is called *Gehenna* in the Greek in Mark 9:45. Between paradise and hell (the two districts of Hades) there was "a great chasm" (Luke 16:26). The fact that no one could cross this chasm indicates that, after death, one's fate is sealed.

Today, when an unbeliever dies, he follows the Old Testament unbelievers to the torment side of Hades. At the final judgment, Hades will be emptied before the great white throne, where its occupants will be judged prior to entering the lake of fire (Revelation 20:13–15).

On the other hand, when a believer dies today, he is "present with the Lord" in heaven (2 Corinthians 5:6–9 NKJV). There, he joins the Old Testament saints who have been enjoying their reward for thousands of years.

A resurrection awaits everyone—either a resurrection to eternal life or a resurrection to "shame and everlasting contempt" (Daniel 12:2). The Bible states that New Testament saints who have died will be resurrected at the event we call the rapture of the church (1 Thessalonians 4:16–17). The Bible is less clear about when the Old Testament saints will be resurrected. It is our view that Old Testament believers will be joined to their resurrected bodies at the end of the tribulation period when Jesus returns to earth to set up His millennial kingdom (Isaiah 26:19; Hosea 13:14).

4. Who will go to heaven?

People have different ideas about heaven. Many have no understanding of God at all but still like to think of heaven as the "better place" where we all go when we die. Ideas about heaven are often no more than vague hopes, on par with "maybe I'll win the lottery someday." Most people don't give heaven much thought until they attend a funeral or a loved one dies. It is popular to refer to heaven as the place where "the good people go." And of course, everyone they know and love is included in the category of "good people."

But the Bible has a lot to say about life after death, and it contradicts popular opinion. John 3:16 says, "For God so loved the world that he gave his one and only Son, that whoever believes in him shall not perish but have eternal life." Then in verse 36, Jesus says, "Whoever believes in the Son has eternal life, but whoever rejects the Son will not see life, for God's wrath remains on them." Hebrews 9:27 also says, "People are destined to die once, and after that to face judgment." According to these verses, everyone dies, but not everyone goes to heaven (see also Matthew 25:46; Romans 6:23; Luke 12:5; Mark 9:43).

God is holy and perfect. Heaven, His dwelling place, is holy and perfect, too (Psalm 68:5; Nehemiah 1:5; Revelation 11:19). According to Romans 3:10, "there is no one righteous, not even one." No one is "good enough" for heaven. The people we call "good" are not good at all compared to the sinless perfection of God. If God allowed sinful humans to enter the perfection of heaven, that place would no longer be perfect. What standard should be used to determine who is "good enough"? God's standard is the only one that counts, and He has already ruled. Romans 3:23 says that "all have sinned and fall short of the glory of God." The payment for that sin is eternal separation from God (Romans 6:23).

Sin must be punished or God is not just (2 Thessalonians 1:6). The judgment we face at death is simply God bringing our accounts up to date and passing sentence on our crimes against Him. We have no way of making our wrongs right. Our good does not outweigh our bad. Just as one drop of arsenic poison in a glass of water contaminates the whole glass, one sin ruins perfection.

So God became man and took our punishment upon Himself. Jesus is God in the flesh. He lived a sinless life of obedience to His Father (Hebrews 4:15). He had no sin, yet at the cross He took our sin and made it His own. Once He paid the price for our sin, we could be declared holy and perfect (2 Corinthians 5:21). When we confess our sin to Him and ask His forgiveness on the basis of Christ's sacrifice, He saves us. It's as if He stamps "Paid in Full" over our debt of sin (Acts 2:38; 3:19; 1 Peter 3:18).

When we stand before God one day, we cannot beg entrance to heaven based on our own merit. We have none to offer. Compared to God's standard of holiness, not one of us is good enough. But Jesus *is* good enough, and by His merit we can enter heaven. First Corinthians 6:9–11 says, "Do you not know that wrongdoers will not inherit the kingdom of God? Do not be deceived: Neither the sexually immoral nor idolaters nor adulterers nor men who have sex with men nor thieves nor the greedy nor drunkards nor slanderers nor swindlers will inherit the kingdom of God. And that is what some of you were. But you were washed, you were sanctified, you were justified in the name of the Lord Jesus Christ and by the Spirit of our God." The sacrifice of Jesus covers it all.

The people who go to heaven are alike in one way: They are sinners who have placed their faith in the Lord Jesus Christ (John 1:12; Acts 16:31; Romans 10:9). They have recognized their need for a Savior and humbly accepted God's offer of forgiveness. They have repented of their old ways of living and set their course to follow Christ (Mark 8:34; John 15:14). They have not attempted to earn God's forgiveness but have served Him gladly from grateful hearts (Psalm 100:2). The kind of faith that saves a soul is one that transforms a life (James 2:26; 1 John 3:9–10) and rests fully on the grace of God.

5. Who will go to hell?

Hell has become a controversial subject in recent years. The rejection of the reality of hell stems from a human inability to reconcile the love of God with eternal punishment or from an outright rejection of God's Word. Even some professing Christians have come to unbiblical conclusions. Some have tried to redefine hell, create an intermediate state not found in Scripture, or deny hell altogether. In doing so, they are ignoring Jesus' warning in Revelation 22:19, "If anyone takes words away from this scroll of prophecy, God will take away from that person any share in the tree of life and in the Holy City, which are described in this scroll."

Hell is mentioned 167 times in the Bible. It is sometimes called Gehenna, Hades, the pit, the abyss, or everlasting punishment (Luke 8:31; 10:15; 2 Thessalonians 1:9). Jesus spoke of heaven and hell as real places (Matthew 13:41–42; 23:33; Mark 9:43–47; Luke 12:5). The story Jesus told about the rich man and Lazarus was an actual event that demonstrated the reality of the two eternal destinations (Luke 16:19–31). Heaven is the dwelling place of God (2 Chronicles 30:27) where Jesus has gone to "prepare a place" for those who love Him (John 14:2). Hell was created for "the devil and his angels" (Matthew 25:41). But because every human being is a sinner, every person deserves hell (Romans 3:10; 5:12; John 3:18). Hell is the just punishment for our rebellion against God (Romans 6:23).

Jesus was clear that "no one can see the kingdom of God unless they are born again" (John 3:3). He was also clear that hell is an eternal punishment for those who do not obey Him (Matthew 25:46). Second Thessalonians 1:8–9 says that in the end God "will punish those who do not know God and do not obey the gospel of our Lord Jesus. They will be punished with everlasting destruction and shut out from the presence of the Lord and from the glory of his might." John the Baptist said about Jesus, "His winnowing fork is in his hand, and he will clear his threshing floor, gathering his wheat into the barn and burning up the chaff with unquenchable fire" (Matthew 3:12).

John 3:18 explains in the simplest terms who will go to heaven and who will go to hell: "Whoever believes in him is not condemned, but whoever does not believe stands condemned already because they have not believed in the name of God's one and only Son." So, those who go to hell are specifically those who do not believe in Jesus' name. To "believe" goes beyond a mental recognition of the truth. To believe in Christ for salvation requires a transfer of allegiance. We stop worshiping ourselves, we forsake our sin, and we begin to worship God with our heart, soul, mind, and strength (Matthew 22:36–37; Mark 12:30).

God desires that every person spend eternity with Him (Matthew 18:14; 2 Peter 3:9), but He honors our decision to accept or reject Him (John 4:14). Anyone who so desires can go to heaven (John 1:12). Jesus already paid the price for our salvation, but we must accept that gift. Heaven is perfect, and God cannot take anyone there who insists on holding on to his or her sin instead of turning to Christ. We must allow Him to cleanse us of our sin and make us righteous in His sight (2 Corinthians 5:21). John 1:10–12 shows us the problem and the solution: "He was in the world, and though the world was made through him, the world did not recognize him. He came to that which was his own, but his own did not receive him. Yet to all who did receive him, to those who believed in his name, he gave the right to become children of God."

We can choose to trust in Jesus' payment for our sin —the result will be heaven—or we can choose to pay for our sins ourselves—the result will be eternity in hell.

6. Will more people go to heaven or to hell?

The question of whether there are more people in heaven or hell is answered by Jesus Himself: "Enter through the narrow gate. For wide is the gate and broad is the road that leads to destruction, and many enter through it. But small is the gate and narrow the road that leads to life, and only a few find it" (Matthew 7:13–14).

Only those who receive Jesus Christ by faith are given the right to become children of God (John 1:12). Jesus said, "I am the way and the truth and the life. No one comes to the Father except through me" (John 14:6). We cannot go to heaven through Mohammed, Buddha, or other false gods of man's making. Eternal life is not for those wanting a cheap and easy way to heaven while continuing to live their own selfish and worldly lives on earth. Jesus only saves those who fully trust in Him as Savior (Acts 4:12).

So, what are these two gates in Matthew 7:13–14? They are the entrance to two different "ways." The wide gate leads to the broad way or road. The small, narrow gate leads to the way that is narrow. The narrow way is the way of the godly, and the broad way is the way of the ungodly. The broad way is the easy way. It is attractive and self-indulgent. It is permissive. It's the inclusive way of the world, with few rules, few restrictions, and fewer requirements. Tolerance of sin is the norm where God's Word is not studied and His standards not followed. This way does not develop or champion spiritual maturity, moral character, commitment, or sacrifice. It involves following "the ways of this world and of the ruler of the kingdom of the air, the spirit who is now at work in those who are disobedient" (Ephesians 2:2). The broad way "appears to be right, but in the end it leads to death" (Proverbs 14:12).

Those who preach a gospel of inclusivity where "all ways lead to heaven" preach an utterly different gospel than the one Jesus preached. The gate of deception, self-centeredness, and pride is the wide gate of the world that leads to hell, not the narrow gate that leads to eternal life. Most people spend their lives following the masses who are on the broad road, doing what everyone else does, and believing what everyone else believes.

The narrow way is the hard way, the demanding way. It is the humble way, and those who travel it recognize that they cannot save themselves and must depend on Jesus Christ alone. It's the way of self-denial and the cross. The fact that few find God's way implies that not many seek to find it. However, God promises that all who seek it diligently will find it: "You will seek me and find me when you seek me with all your heart" (Jeremiah 29:13). No one will stumble into the kingdom or wander through the narrow gate by accident. Someone once asked Jesus, "Lord, are only a few people going to be saved?" He replied, "Make every effort to enter through the narrow door, because many, I tell you, will try to enter and will not be able to" (Luke 13:23–24).

Many will desire to have the benefits of that narrow door, the door of salvation, but "will not be able." They are unwilling to trust Jesus alone. They are unwilling to give up the world and its attractions. The way of Christ is the way of the cross, and the way of the cross is the way of self-denial. Jesus said, "Whoever wants to be my disciple must deny themselves and take up their cross daily and follow me. For whoever wants to save their life will lose it, but whoever loses their life for me will save it" (Luke 9:23–24).

Jesus knows that many will choose the wide gate and the broad way that leads to destruction and hell. And He said that only a few will choose the narrow gate. According to Matthew 7:13–14, there is no doubt that more people will go to hell than to heaven. The question for you, then, is "Which road are you on?"

7. Will there be a second chance for salvation after death?

While the idea of a second chance for salvation after death is appealing, the Bible says that death is the end of all chances. According to Hebrews 9:27, when we die, we then face judgment. So, as long as a person is alive, he has a "second chance" to accept Christ and be saved—and a third, fourth, fifth, etc., chance (see

John 3:16; Romans 10:9–10; Acts 16:31). Once a person dies, however, there are no more chances.

Only faith in Christ can save us, and all who reject this salvation will go to eternal punishment. Revelation 20:11–15, which describes the final judgment, provides some insight into the finality of our decision to follow or reject Christ. At the great white throne, record books are opened. All whose names are not found in the Lamb's Book of Life (Revelation 21:27) are condemned to the lake of fire. Those who are not in the book of life have rejected Christ's offer of salvation and are judged according to their own deeds. Revelation 20:12 says that "the dead were judged according to what they had done as recorded in the books."

Not even a person's "good" deeds and law-keeping will avail without faith in Christ, for "no one will be declared righteous in God's sight by the works of the law" (Romans 3:20). Therefore, all who are judged according to their own works are condemned to hell. All have broken the law at some point—no one measures up to God's standard of holiness. Believers in Christ, on the other hand, are not judged the same way because their names are written in the book of life. These are the ones who have believed on the Lord Jesus. Jesus paid the penalty for their sin and fulfilled the requirements of the law on their behalf, and they alone will be allowed to enter heaven.

Concerning those who die in a state of unbelief, wouldn't they repent and believe if they were given a second chance in hell? The answer is no, they would not. The heart is not changed simply because a person dies. The heart and mind are still at enmity against God, even in hell. In the story of the rich man and Lazarus in Luke 16:19–31, the rich man is in torment in hell. But he does not repent. He does not ask for a second chance. He only asks that Abraham send Lazarus back to earth to warn his brothers so they wouldn't have to suffer the same fate. There was no repentance in his heart, only regret for where he found himself. Abraham's answer is notable: "If they do not listen to Moses and the Prophets, they will not be convinced even if someone rises from the dead" (Luke 16:31). In other words, the witness of the Scriptures is sufficient for salvation for everyone alive, and no other revelation will bring salvation to those who refuse to hear.

No one goes to hell because he or she did not have enough chances to be saved. No one needs a "second chance" once he is in hell. We trust the goodness and wisdom of God, that He gives sufficient light to everyone to believe. Jesus is "the true light that gives light to everyone" (John 1:9). If a person fails to trust Christ before he dies, then he would *not* have come to Christ even if he had lived longer. God knows exactly what we need—including how many chances we need to hear the gospel. In His mercy, God gives every person ample time and sufficient opportunity to be saved.

One day, everyone will bow before Jesus and recognize that He is the Lord and Savior (Philippians 2:10–11). At that point, though, it will be too late for salvation. After death, all that remains for the unbeliever is judgment (Revelation 20:14–15). For this reason, we must trust in Jesus in *this* life. "I tell you, now is the time of God's favor, now is the day of salvation" (2 Corinthians 6:2).

SECTION 2
Questions about Death

8. What does the Bible say about death?

The Bible presents death as separation: Physical death is the separation of the soul from the body, and spiritual death is the separation of the soul from God.

Death is the result of sin. "For the wages of sin is death" (Romans 6:23). The whole world is subject to death because all have sinned. "Sin entered the world through one man, and death through sin, and in this way death came to all people, because all sinned" (Romans 5:12). In Genesis 2:17, the Lord warned Adam that the penalty for disobedience would be death—"You will certainly die." When Adam disobeyed, he experienced immediate spiritual death, which caused him to hide "from the Lord God among the trees of the garden" (Genesis 3:8). Later, Adam experienced physical death (Genesis 5:5).

On the cross, Jesus also experienced physical death (Matthew 27:50). The difference is that Adam died because he was a sinner, and Jesus, who had never sinned, chose to die as a substitute for sinners (Hebrews 2:9). Jesus then showed His power over death and sin by rising from the dead on the third day (Matthew 28; Revelation 1:18). Because of Christ, death is a defeated foe. "O death, where is thy sting? O grave, where is thy victory?" (1 Corinthians 15:55 KJV; cf. Hosea 13:14).

For the unsaved, death ends the chance to accept God's gracious offer of salvation: "People are destined to die once, and after that to face judgment" (Hebrews 9:27). For the saved, death ushers them into the presence of Christ, "to be absent from the body and to be present with the Lord" (2 Corinthians 5:8 NKJV; cf. Philippians 1:23). So real is the promise of the believer's resurrection that the physical death of a Christian is called "sleep" (1 Corinthians 15:51; 1 Thessalonians 5:10). We look forward to that time when "there will be no more death" (Revelation 21:4).

9. Do we have an appointed time of death?

The Bible says that "all the days ordained for me were written in your book before one of them came to be" (Psalm 139:16). God knows absolutely everything about us (Psalm 139:1–6) including when, where, and how we will die. So, yes, it does seem that we have an appointed time of death.

In Job's suffering-fueled complaint against God, he mentions God's role in the timing of our death:

> A person's days are determined;
> you have decreed the number of his months
> and have set limits he cannot exceed.
>
> Job 14:5

Or, as the New Living Translation puts it,

> You have decided the length of our lives.
> You know how many months we will live,
> and we are not given a minute longer.

According to this verse, the length of our lives is decreed by God, who has determined our days. A person has "set limits" on how long he lives on earth. No one is able to change God's decree, and no one has the power to extend his life beyond what God has decided.

An important note is that none of us know the time of our death. Such knowledge is God's alone. The one exception may be the miracle God performed for King Hezekiah in Isaiah 38. The king was sick "and was at the point of death" (Isaiah 38:1). In great sorrow, Hezekiah prayed, and the Lord answered through the prophet Isaiah: "Go and tell Hezekiah, 'This is what the LORD, the God of your father David, says: I have heard your prayer and seen your tears; I will add fifteen years to your life'" (verse 5). This is the only time that we know of when anyone learned how long he would live. It also seems to be the only instance of God's prolonging a life. The uniqueness of this miracle is brought out by the startling sign that accompanied it—the shadow on the sundial moved backward (verses 7–8).

God is sovereign, and He has mapped out our lives. This would include an appointed time of death. At the same time, based on King Hezekiah's story, it is not wrong to pray for life to be prolonged, for disease to be removed, and for health to be extended.

Since we do not know the number of our days, we should live each day for God. James 4:13–15 gives some practical wisdom on this matter: "Now listen, you who say, 'Today or tomorrow we will go to this or that city, spend a year there, carry on business and make money.' Why, you do not even know what will happen tomorrow. What is your life? You are a mist that appears for a little while and then vanishes. Instead, you ought to say, 'If it is the Lord's will, we will live and do this or that.'" We should make wise decisions about how we live and how we take care of ourselves. And, ultimately, we trust God's sovereignty in all things, including our time of death.

10. How can I overcome the fear of death? How can I stop being scared of dying?

Even the most secure, devout believer can have occasions when he fears death. It is hard-wired into our systems to avoid death. Death was not an original part of God's plan for His creation. We were made to be whole and holy, living in paradise in communion with Him. The introduction of death was a necessary response to the admittance of sin into the world. In a sense, it is a grace that we die. If we didn't, we would have to live in a sinful world for all eternity.

Even with the knowledge that death serves a purpose, we have a visceral reaction to the thought of our own mortality. The fragility of our physical bodies and the sudden cessation of life are stark reminders of our lack of control in a large and dangerous world. We do have the great hope that He who is in us is greater than he who is in the world (1 John 4:4), and the One who loves us did go to prepare a place for us so we could join Him someday (John 14:2). But, in overcoming a fear of death, it might help to consider some immediate, practical considerations.

First, what is the actual fear that we face? There are several aspects of death that can potentially cause fear. Fortunately, God has an answer for each of them.

Fear of the unknown

What exactly does it feel like to die? What can you see as your life leaves your physical body? How will it come about? Is it anything like people have reported—a bright light? A group of relatives?

No one knows for certain what it feels like to die, but the Bible does describe what happens. Second Corinthians 5:6–8 and Philippians 1:23 say that, when we leave our body, we are at home with the Lord. What a reassuring thought! Then we have the promise of bodily resurrection, at which time we will be given new, glorified bodies (1 Corinthians 15:20–22; 6:14).

Fear of loss of control

By the time humans reach adulthood, they have a pretty good idea how to interact with the world around them. They know how to find what they need, get to where they want to be, and interact with others in a way that fulfills their intent.

Many, though, even those who profess a trust in God, are so fearful of not getting what they need that they try to manipulate their surroundings and the people around them to their benefit. Some abuse others and take advantage of them, grasping for control. They don't trust God to provide for their needs, so they take care of things themselves. They don't trust others to give them consideration, so they demand what they think they need.

These people must certainly fear the loss of control upon their deaths. The apostle Peter showed a fear of death when he denied Jesus three times. Later, Jesus forgave Peter and encouraged him in service. After Jesus returned to heaven, Peter was filled with the Holy Spirit, and all fear of death was gone. His passion for boldly preaching Christ's message far outstripped his need to control his surroundings (Acts 5:17–42). The Holy Spirit alone gave Peter the strength to endure the challenges he would face.

Fear for those left behind

The Christian view of death is that it involves separation. Ultimate death is eternal separation from God. In physical death, we are separated from our bodies and from our loved ones on earth for a time. If our loved ones are also believers, we know that the separation will be a blink of the eye compared to eternity in heaven. If they are not believers, the separation will be permanent. Our mission, then, is to use our time together to pray for our loved ones and talk to them about eternity. Ultimately, we commit our loved ones into God's hands.

Fear of the act of dying

Few ever know how they will die. Some deaths are quick and painless; others face a long, drawn-out illness. The mystery surrounding death and, in most cases, the inability to prepare for it can be frightening. Even if we do know the manner of our death—we've been diagnosed with a terminal illness, for example—we must still overcome certain fears.

But death itself is only a moment in time—a moment nearly everyone has experienced or will. When that moment is over, we will claim Philippians 3:20–21: "But our citizenship is in heaven. And we eagerly await a Savior from there, the Lord Jesus Christ, who, by the power that enables him to bring everything under his control, will transform our lowly bodies so that they will be like his glorious body."

Often, being informed of and actively participating in matters related to our own end of life can help assuage fear. You can take steps to prepare yourself and those around you.

Overcoming the fear of death—Practical steps

Many people believe they shouldn't die because they have too much to live for. Often, this means they have responsibilities and unfinished business that would be neglected if they were gone. Doing what you can *now* to make sure your responsibilities and tasks are taken care of *then* can alleviate fear.

If you have a business or children or other dependents, consider their care. Decide who will take over your role, and work with that person to come up with a plan. Prepare a will or a trust. Make sure all your necessary paperwork is organized and easy to find.

Reconcile broken relationships while you can. But don't live for dying. Just take reasonable steps to put things in order.

Overcoming the fear of death—Legal steps

Part of planning ahead involves deciding what will happen in the event you become incapacitated. It's possible that, during the course of an illness or injury, you'll lose control of the situation and be unable to make your wishes known. To prevent confusion and possible turmoil, many people opt to set up an advance directive such as a living will or power of attorney. At any rate, it's wise to let those closest to you know what you want—at least tell them where it's written down.

Overcoming the fear of death—Spiritual steps

The most important thing to remember regarding death is the truth about life. You love your family and care for them, but God loves them more. You may worry about your earthly legacy, but God is more concerned with an eternal, kingdom perspective. All the paperwork in the world won't bring the peace of mind that comes with abiding in Christ.

Living in this world, it's difficult to keep in mind that this is just a temporary condition. First John 2:15–17 helps us to maintain the proper perspective: "Do not love the world or anything in the world. If anyone loves the world, love for the Father is not in them. For everything in the world—the lust of the flesh, the lust of the eyes, and the pride of life—comes not from the Father but from the world. The world and its desires pass away, but whoever does the will of God lives forever." Staying in the truth of God's Word and believing what He says about us and the world around us will give us the proper perspective and take away fear.

In overcoming the fear of death, we cling to 1 John 3:1–2: "See what great love the Father has lavished on us, that we should be called children of God! And that is what we are! The reason the world does not know us is that it did not know him. Dear friends, now we are children of God, and what we will be has not yet been made known. But we know that when Christ appears, we shall be like him, for we shall see him as he is."

11. How can I be prepared to die?

Death and dying are uncomfortable subjects for most people, particularly when it comes to one's own death. Many of us make our way through life never giving a thought to our mortality until a serious illness, the loss of a loved one, or some other jarring occasion confronts us with the inescapable reality that one day we will die. Ecclesiastes 7:2 tells us that "death is the destiny of everyone; the living should take this to heart." How do I take to heart the fact of my own death? How can I be prepared to die?

Scripture calls death an enemy (1 Corinthians 15:26). Because of death's finality and because so much about it is unknown, it's not unusual for us to feel anxious about death and have some fear of dying. But the Bible teaches that Jesus Christ has destroyed the enemy of death once and for all: "Now with the coming of our Savior Christ Jesus, he has . . . destroyed death, and through the Good News he has brought eternal life into full view" (2 Timothy 1:10 GW). Those who have trusted Jesus Christ for salvation need not fear death but can have full assurance and confidence in facing the grave.

The Bible is clear that after death comes judgment (Hebrews 9:27), but most people are not ready to "meet their Maker." The first and foremost way to prepare for death is to be sure we are in a right relationship with God. Having a right relationship with God starts with acknowledging our sin before Him and seeking His forgiveness. It means placing our faith in Jesus Christ as Lord and Savior: "If you openly declare that Jesus is Lord and believe in your heart that God raised him from the dead, you will be saved" (Romans 10:9 NLT). Salvation is God's gift to us (Ephesians 2:8); we only need to receive it by faith.

A right relationship with God through Jesus Christ frees us from the penalty of sin (1 Thessalonians 1:10; Romans 8:1–2; Hebrews 9:15) and from death itself (1 Corinthians 15:22–23; Romans 5:12–17; 7:24). It also liberates us from the fear of dying: "Because God's children are human beings—made of flesh and blood—the Son also became flesh and blood. For only as a human being could he die, and only by dying could he break the power of the devil, who had the power of death. Only in this way could he set free all who have lived their lives as slaves to the fear of dying" (Hebrews 2:14–15 NLT).

The sting of death is removed for Christians because we know where we are going when we die. Our perishing bodies will be transformed into immortal ones that will live forever with Christ in God's eternal kingdom (1 Corinthians 15:42–58). In reality, we are not ready to live until we are prepared to die.

After we have placed our faith in Jesus Christ for salvation, we can further prepare for death by staying in right relationship with the people in our lives. We ought to consider our relationships with family members, friends, neighbors, and coworkers. Are there any relationships that need to be reconciled? Is there someone we need to forgive or someone we need to ask for forgiveness? Are there words that need to be said?

Concerning practical ways to prepare, we ought to realistically consider the financial impact our death will have on our family and do our best to plan ahead. Do we need to draw up a will or other legal documents, purchase life insurance, or set aside funds for funeral and burial expenses? Another thoughtful arrangement is to leave written instructions for our memorial service.

Scripture teaches us to live with an awareness of our death and cultivate an eternal perspective. We should invest our time, talents, and resources in things that have everlasting value. Jesus described this eternal mindset as daily dying for Him: "If any of you wants to be my follower, you must give up your own way, take up your cross daily, and follow me. If you try to hang on to your life, you will lose it. But if you give up your life for my sake, you will save it" (Luke 9:23–24 NLT). Believers live with the hope of heaven and a readiness to lay down their lives for Jesus.

Death for the believer is the beginning of a new, eternal phase of life. When our days on earth come to an end, we will transition to the beginning of a heavenly life. Heaven is our true home where God waits to welcome us into His arms. In His eternal kingdom, all heartache, pain, and death will cease (Revelation 21:4). We will enjoy intimate fellowship with God and our loved ones. No matter how spectacular we imagine heaven will be, the Bible promises it will be even better: "No eye has seen, no ear has heard, and no mind has imagined the things that God has prepared for those who love him" (1 Corinthians 2:9 GW).

12. How do I find comfort and peace when I have lost a loved one to death?

If you have lost a loved one to death, you know what a painful experience it is. Jesus understood the pain of losing someone close to His heart. In the book of John (11:1–44), we learn that Jesus lost a loved one named Lazarus. Jesus was deeply moved and wept at the loss of His friend. This story, however, doesn't end in tears. Jesus knew He possessed the power to raise Lazarus from the dead. Jesus said, "I am the resurrection and the life. The one who believes in me will live, even though they die; and whoever lives by believing in me will never die" (John 11:25–26). It is comforting to know that death is not the end for those who believe in Christ. Those who know Jesus as Savior will have eternal life (John 10:28). God has prepared a new home for us where there will be no more death, tears, or pain (Revelation 21:1–4).

The knowledge that our loved one is in heaven brings comfort, but we still experience the pain of their absence. It is okay to grieve the loss of your loved one. Jesus wept over the death of

Lazarus, even knowing He would bring Lazarus back to life. God does not despise our emotions or our questions. We can cast our burdens on Him and trust in His love to provide us reassurance and comfort (1 Peter 5:7).

As part of the healing process, we can remember the many good things about our lost loved ones and rejoice in the fact that we were able to share in their lives. We can share stories about the impact our lost loved ones have had on our lives. We might find it comforting to do some of the things our lost loved ones particularly enjoyed or to spend time reminiscing about our lost loved ones with others. We can also honor their memory by living our lives in a way that brings honor and glory to God.

God is ultimately the source of our comfort (2 Corinthians 7:6). It is good to remember our lost loved ones and to honor their influence in our lives, but we are not to pray to them or seek to communicate with them in any way. Instead, we bring our prayers to God and ask Him for comfort and healing. God is the father of compassion, and He will comfort us in all our troubles (2 Corinthians 1:3–4). Be assured that God loves you and that He understands how much you are hurting. Run to the shelter of the Most High, where you will find sweet rest (Psalm 91:1–2).

13. How should Christian parents handle the death of a child?

As parents, we cannot imagine a more traumatic experience than the death of a child. All parents naturally expect their children to outlive them. Such a loss is an extraordinary, out-of-order event that brings with it an overwhelming sense of pain and lingering grief. It is a life-altering experience that presents unique challenges to parents as they seek to rebuild their lives without their child.

It would be presumptuous for anyone to tell parents how to handle the death of a child. However, we do know that those who yield their lives to God are more apt to recover from such a loss with a greater sense of normalcy than those without a genuine and positive faith in our Creator. This being true, how do Christian parents handle the death of a child? Does the Bible address the subject, and if so, in what way?

First, we should note that each person handles grief differently. Emotions are normal and natural, but they vary widely in intensity and expression. Second, no parent ever "gets over" or "moves on" from the death of a child. It's not like an illness from which we recover. Most counselors liken it to a life-changing physical injury. However, we should also know that, though we may always feel the loss, its intensity does diminish with time.

It is faith in a loving and ever-faithful God that enables us to endure and recover from the death of a child, sometimes in ways that others find remarkable. Such was the case of David in the loss of his child who died seven days after birth (2 Samuel 12:18–19). There are several valuable lessons we can learn from this passage of Scripture that can help grieving parents to face the future with hope.

One is that, before the child died, David prayed fervently for his child's life (2 Samuel 12:16). This should be true for all parents at all times, not just when times are difficult. Parents should always pray for their children, asking God to watch over and protect them. Likewise, parents should pray for God to provide wisdom and guidance so their children will grow in the nurture and admonition of the Lord (Judges 13:12; Proverbs 22:6; Ephesians 6:4).

David's reaction to his child's death contains another lesson. Upon learning that the infant had died, David immediately accepted the fact and began a return to normalcy: "David arose from the ground, washed and anointed himself, and changed his clothes; and he went into the house of the LORD and worshiped. Then he went to his own house; and when he requested, they set food before him, and he ate" (2 Samuel 12:20 NKJV). What may surprise us most about this passage is that David "went into the house of the LORD and worshiped." In other words, David not only accepted the death of his child, but he gave all his emotions and the reality of the situation to God. Through it all, he saw God as worthy of worship. The ability to worship and honor God in a time of trial or crisis is a powerful demonstration of our spiritual confidence in God. Worship enables us to accept the reality of our loss. And this is how God frees us to go on living. What David models for us is learning to turn loose what we cannot change.

The next lesson in David's story is the most revealing. It is what appears to be confidence in the knowledge that children who die before they reach the age of accountability go to heaven. David's attendants questioned his reaction to the death of his child, and David's response has always been a source of comfort to believing parents who have lost infants and young children: "Now that he is dead, why should I go on fasting? Can I bring him back again? I will go to him, but he will not return to me" (2 Samuel 12:23). David was fully confident that he would meet his son in heaven. This passage is a powerful indication that babies and young children who pass from this world will go to heaven.

Grieving the death of a child is a heartrending journey. There are no hard-and-fast rules to teach us how to handle our mourning. However, counselors and those who have experienced the loss of a child have provided some helpful advice:

- Recognize that you are not alone. You have God. You have your brothers and sisters in Christ. You have close friends and family. Lean on them. They are there to help you.
- Don't put time limits on your recovery. Don't expect a day to pass without thinking about your child. Welcome such thoughts.
- Talk about your child. It's important that you share the story of your child with others.
- Take care of yourself.

- Take care of your other children. They, too, are suffering.
  They grieve the loss of a sibling and have the additional
  discomfort of seeing their parents in grief.
- Try not to make any major decisions for at least the first
  year.
- Expect that getting through the many "firsts" following the
  death of a young child will be painful—first birthday, first
  Christmas, etc.

And last, Christians who have experienced the death of a child have
the grand and faithful promise of God's Word: "And God shall wipe
away all tears from their eyes; and there shall be no more death,
neither sorrow, nor crying, neither shall there be any more pain:
for the former things are passed away" (Revelation 21:4 KJV).

14. How can I find comfort when an unsaved loved one has died?

For the believer, the death of an unsaved loved one is tragic and difficult to process. In some cases, it seems we will never find comfort
or peace of mind when we know the destiny awaiting the unsaved.

When a saved loved one dies, we miss him or her, but we do
not grieve "as others who have no hope" (1 Thessalonians 4:13
NKJV) because we know we will be reunited in heaven one day. But
when loved ones die without Christ, we know we will not see them
again, and finding comfort in that situation may seem hopeless.

Believers who have taken pains to communicate gospel truths
to their loved ones feel an additional pain that asks "why?" As
Christians, we wonder how anyone could refuse a gift as precious
as salvation. Our joy in the Lord moves us to want that same joy
for others. But the truth is that, even though the invitation is open
to all, not all will receive the gift. We can take comfort that, even
though we may never see our unsaved loved ones again, God is

always faithful and just. God gave them the opportunity to turn to Him. God is so patient, and He leaves the door open for so long. "Will not the Judge of all the earth do right?" (Genesis 18:25). The answer is, of course, that God *does* do what is right, and this is a great comfort to those who are unsure of the destination of a loved one's soul. God is a sovereign judge of righteousness. He is full of grace and mercy to all who call upon Him. It is His very justice that offers a way for all to escape judgment, and it is in that justice that we must rest. It is grace that saves us, and it is grace in which we stand when we go through the double grief of the death of an unsaved loved one. We yearn for the unsaved to choose Christ, but some will not. Those who have passed into eternity without Christ have made their choice, but it was God's grace that gave them a choice to begin with.

Although we may have pain in the remembrance of that loved one, there will come a time when each born-again believer will be with the Lord. In that day "God shall wipe away all tears from their eyes; and there shall be no more death, neither sorrow, nor crying, neither shall there be any more pain: for the former things are passed away" (Revelation 21:4 KJV). Even if we cannot comprehend such a time, the promise should be enough to bring comfort and encouragement. When we see the Lord, the sorrow we have now will disappear: "Now is your time of grief, but I will see you again and you will rejoice, and no one will take away your joy" (John 16:22). As we wait for the day when sorrow will be no more, we can lean on the everlasting arms of God, who feels our pain and comforts us with His great love and mercy.

15. Can people in heaven look down and see us?

Some see in Hebrews 12:1 the idea that people in heaven might be able to look down and see us: "Therefore, since we are surrounded by such a great cloud of witnesses . . ." The "witnesses" are the heroes of faith listed in Hebrews 11, and the fact that we are "surrounded" by them leads some commentators to understand that those heroes (and possibly other people) are looking down on us from heaven.

The idea that people are looking down from heaven to see what we're doing is common in popular culture. But, as much as we might like the notion that we're being watched by our departed loved ones, that's not what Hebrews 12:1 is teaching. Building on Hebrews 11, the author begins drawing up some practical lessons (that's why chapter 12 begins with "Therefore"). The "witnesses" are the people whom God commends for their faith in chapter 11, and there is a large crowd of them in heaven. The question is, in what way are they "witnesses"?

The proper interpretation of Hebrews 12:1 is that the men and women forming the "great cloud," or crowd, bear witness to the value of living life by faith. Their Old Testament stories give testimony to the blessings of choosing faith over fear. To paraphrase the start of Hebrews 12:1, "Since we have so many tried-and-true examples of proven faith . . ." So, it's not that people are in heaven watching us (as if our lives on earth are so interesting or they have nothing better to do!) but that those who have gone before us have set a lasting example for us. The record of their lives bears witness to faith and God and truth.

Hebrews 12:1 continues, "Let us throw off everything that hinders and the sin that so easily entangles. And let us run with perseverance the race marked out for us." Because of the faith and endurance of believers who went before us, we are inspired to stay the course in our own race of faith. We follow the examples of Abraham, Moses, Rahab, Gideon, and others.

Some people point to the rich man's mention of his brothers in Luke 16:28 as proof that departed souls (in Hades, at least) can see events on earth. However, the passage never says the rich man could *see* his brothers or knew of their activities; rather, he remembered he had brothers, and he knew they were unbeliev-ers. Also, some people use Revelation 6:10 as a proof text: the tribulation martyrs call for God to avenge their deaths. Again, this passage says nothing about the martyrs *seeing* people on earth; it simply says they remembered the injustice they had suffered and desired the Lord to take action.

The Bible doesn't specifically say that people in heaven *cannot* look down on us, so we can't be dogmatic. However, it is unlikely that they can. People in heaven are likely occupied with other things, such as worshiping God and enjoying the glories of heaven.

Whether or not people in heaven can look down and see us, we are not running our race for them. We are not hoping for their approval or listening for their applause. Hebrews 12:2 keeps our focus where it belongs: "Fixing our eyes on Jesus, the pioneer and perfecter of faith." Jesus is our blessed hope, no other (Titus 2:13).

16. Can I ask God to deliver a message to a loved one who has died?

Some people who have lost loved ones deeply desire to speak with them again. Some wonder if it is okay to ask God to give a message to their loved one in heaven. To be clear, there is no specific Bible verse that speaks directly for or against this idea. However, there are some biblical principles to consider.

First, Scripture says we are not to attempt to communicate with the spirits of the dead. According to Old Testament law, at-tempting to do so was punishable by death (Deuteronomy 18:11). God judged Saul for this practice (1 Samuel 28). Since we are not to speak with spirits or attempt to contact the dead, it is wrong to pray directly to departed loved ones. It would also seem that asking God to speak to the spirits of loved ones on our behalf is neither helpful nor necessary.

Second, there's no need to relay messages to people in heaven because those loved ones who are now with the Lord are not separated from us forever. Believers will one day reunite with loved ones in heaven. Instead of attempting to communicate a message to them now, we can look forward to something much better—seeing them again face-to-face in the presence of the Lord. Revelation 21:4 promises that in the end, "'He will wipe every tear from their eyes. There will be no more death' or mourning or crying or pain, for the old order of things has passed away."

Third, we can always come to God with our hurts and pains, knowing He perfectly understands how we feel. When we lose a loved one, the pain can be overwhelming. We may want to communicate with the person or reconnect in some way because things are just not the same without him or her. God calls us to turn to Him in these times of pain. He is our comforter and healer. When we trust in Him, He can provide the help we need to carry on despite the painful loss of a loved one. We can rest assured that God is comforting our loved ones in heaven with a perfect consolation; any supposed comfort they may derive from our personal messages would pale in comparison.

It does not seem fitting to ask Jesus to be our telephone operator or personal courier. After all, He has already promised believers will be together again someday. It is best to deal with separation from our loved ones in a way that honors Christ and gives Him all glory. There is no reason to ask God to deliver messages to loved ones in heaven.

17. What does it mean to be absent from the body?

The phrase *absent from the body* is found in 2 Corinthians 5:8. Paul states that he is confident in his eternal destiny and longs for the day when he can be "absent from the body" (NKJV) and be present with the Lord he loves and serves. To be "absent" from one's body simply means to die because, at death, the spirit is separated from the body and moves to another place—either heaven with the Lord or hell, separated from God for eternity.

Like Paul, Christians can always be "confident and know that as long as we are at home in the body we are away from the Lord. For we live by faith, not by sight. We are confident . . . and would prefer to be away from the body and at home with the Lord" (2 Corinthians 5:6–8). When a born-again believer dies, his soul goes immediately into the presence of the Lord. There, the soul consciously awaits the resurrection of the body. To the church at Philippi, Paul wrote this from a Roman prison:

> For to me, to live is Christ, and to die is gain. But if I live on in the flesh, this will mean fruit from my labor; yet what I shall choose I cannot tell. For I am hard-pressed between the two, having a desire to depart and be with Christ, which is far better. Nevertheless to remain in the flesh is more needful for you.
>
> Philippians 1:21–24 NKJV

Paul's desire in life was to glorify the Lord Jesus Christ. If he lived, he could continue to labor for the Lord. If he faced execution, he would depart this life and be with Christ. He desired to be with his Savior, but if he remained on earth, he could continue to minister to others.

There are some who believe in soul sleep, the doctrine that, when a person dies, his body and soul sleep in the grave, awaiting the resurrection. But if this were true, why would Paul not want to live to minister as long as possible, rather than sleep in a grave? And if it were true that the body and soul are never separated, it would be impossible to ever be absent from the body and present with the Lord.

We conclude, then, that believers who die are indeed absent from their physical bodies and present with the Lord in conscious bliss awaiting that grand resurrection day!

18. Is God sovereign over death?

We know that God knows the exact number of our days (Psalm 39:4). He does not share that knowledge with us, as it would not be good for us to know. The day of our death is one of "the secret things [that] belong to the LORD our God" (Deuteronomy 29:29). We also know that, being sovereign, God is in control of the day of our death.

Some circumstances, such as murder, give rise to questions about God's sovereignty over death. A murderer seemingly cuts short the number of a person's days. Has the murderer successfully wrested control from God and determined for himself the time and manner of someone's death? If so—if the murderer overpowered the will of God—then God was not sovereign over death in that instance. We reject that conclusion. But then we are faced with another question: If God remained sovereign, then did He *cause* the murder? The tension between the sovereignty of God and the free will of man becomes evident.

We must understand that God's sovereignty is not incompatible with the actions of human agents (including evil actions). Several passages of Scripture bear this out—see Genesis 50:20 and Luke 22:22. In His perfect knowledge, God can know the exact number of our days. In His sovereignty, He can even determine that number. At the same time, He can allow for the actions of evil people without being the cause of evil. His plan will be accomplished, even as "the power of darkness" is given its "hour" in which to work (Luke 22:53 ESV).

God's sovereignty means He is in absolute control over all things (Colossians 1:16–17; Psalm 90:2; 1 Chronicles 29:11–12). Nothing can affect or hinder God. In the most basic sense, God causes all things to be (Hebrews 1:3). By His eternal decree everything else exists and has its being. There is a radically contingent nature to all things outside of God. Even the subatomic particles comprising individual physical objects (and the circumstances to which they pertain) must be made to exist, and God is the cause of their existence.

Yet this does not mean God *deterministically* causes all things. An engineer who designs a machine can follow one of two paths. Either he can allow the machine to function with foreknown variations, or he can interfere to "force" a certain event. In either case, the engineer is in total control—he is "sovereign" over the machine he made. In only the latter case, however, is the engineer the deterministic cause of the event.

The fact that God is sovereign means He is entirely beyond the power of any other influence—He cannot be "stopped" or overcome in any way, shape, or form. That does not mean that God "must" do certain things. He is free. God's sovereignty is related to but separate from His omnipotence. Omnipotence is the power to do anything that power can accomplish. Sovereignty is the absolute, unfettered right to decide when and how—and *if*—to use that power.

In other words, God's sovereignty allows Him to *not* act—to *allow*—just as much as it allows Him to act. The choice to act or not to act is part of His sovereign nature. So, God can "allow" certain things to occur and not be a deterministic cause of those events. Yet all these things are under His sovereign control (Ephesians 1:11). According to His sovereign choice, God has willed that events come to pass in accordance with the nature/essence of moral agents. Some of those events God simply "allows," knowing as He does that everything will ultimately lead to His intended conclusion. Thus, God can will events to come to pass—either directly or indirectly—using the non-coerced, freely willed acts of responsible moral agents.

The importance of God sovereignly "allowing" actions cannot be overstated. God's providing the "setting" for an act to occur does not mean He is a responsible moral agent for the act. The moral responsibility for intentionally evil acts falls on those who themselves commit the acts. Evil is like rust in metal or rot in a tree. God "causes" the tree and thus provides the setting that "enables" the rot. But, in this analogy, God does not make the rot. God knows the tree will rot, He "allows" the tree to rot, and He chooses not to stop the rotting process, all for His own purpose—perhaps knowing the rot will prevent a greater disease later on. In a similar way, God does not make evil, although He "allows" a certain amount of it for His own purposes. He keeps His own counsel in such matters.

God knows things by virtue of His own nature. In a simple eternal act, God perfectly knows Himself. By knowing Himself, God knows all that He causes. Because the nature of God is immutable (Malachi 3:6), the concepts of "before" and "after" do not apply to Him. God's knowledge is not temporal, sequential, or time-bound. In comparison, consider a piece of sheet music. The song inscribed on the page is bound to the two dimensions of symbols and paper. But the person who wrote the music is bound neither by those dimensions nor the "tempo" of the song. The composer can see and understand all of his composition at once, without restriction. He can change what he wants in the music—or not change it, as he desires. In a similar way, that which is past and future to us is eternally present to God. God does not "foreknow" things as we might say of a prophet; God simply *knows*.

Human beings, as free moral agents, act without extrinsic moral coercion. And it is God who causes humans to have that freedom to act. God knows all mankind's choices in advance and either "allows" them or interferes with them as He sees fit. Through it all, humans are held responsible for the choices they make.

So, God wills that man make non-deterministic moral choices. Since God's knowledge is not time-bound, He knows when a person will die and how that person will die. A person's death falls within God's sovereign control. We can say that God wills all events in an existentially basic, causal way, but not all of them in a *morally* causal way. It is possible for God to "allow" acts that He would not directly cause or even prefer (Matthew 23:37). A human being acting with malice is fully culpable from a moral standpoint; God cannot be the substantial or accidental cause of evil.

Properly distinguishing between God "knowing," God "allowing," and God "causing" helps us understand the normative predication of both human and divine action.

SECTION 3

Questions about the Afterlife

19. Is there an afterlife?

Jesus Christ is the one person who can speak with real authority (and experience) concerning the afterlife. What gives Him sole authority to speak of heaven is that He came from there: "No one has ever gone into heaven except the one who came from heaven—the Son of Man" (John 3:13). The Lord Jesus, with His firsthand experience in heaven, presents us with three basic truths about life after death:

1. There is an afterlife.
2. When a person dies, there are two possible destinations to which he or she may go.
3. There is one way to ensure a positive experience after death.

Christ affirms there is an afterlife a number of times. For example, in an encounter with the Sadducees, who denied the doctrine of the resurrection, Jesus said, "About the dead rising—have you not read in the Book of Moses, in the account of the burning bush, how God said to him, 'I am the God of Abraham, the God of Isaac, and the God of Jacob'? He is not the God of the dead, but of the living. You are badly mistaken!" (Mark 12:26–27). According to Jesus, those who had died centuries before were very much alive with God at that moment.

In another passage, Jesus comforts His disciples (and us) by telling them of the afterlife. They can look forward to being with Him in heaven: "Do not let your hearts be troubled. You believe in God; believe also in me. My Father's house has many rooms; if that were not so, would I have told you that I am going there to prepare a place for you? And if I go and prepare a place for you, I will come back and take you to be with me that you also may be where I am" (John 14:1–3).

Jesus also speaks authoritatively about the two different destinies that await in the afterlife. Relating the account of the rich man and Lazarus, Jesus says, "The time came when the beggar died and the angels carried him to Abraham's side. The rich man also died and was buried. In Hades, where he was in torment, he looked up and saw Abraham far away, with Lazarus by his side" (Luke 16:22–23). Note that there is no purgatory for those who die; they go directly to their eternal destiny. Jesus taught more on the different destinies of the righteous and the wicked in Matthew 25:46 and John 5:25–29.

Jesus also emphasized that what determines a person's eternal destination is faith in God's only begotten Son. The need for faith is clear: "Everyone who believes may have eternal life in him. For God so loved the world that he gave his one and only Son, that whoever believes in him shall not perish but have eternal life. For God did not send his Son into the world to condemn the world, but to save the world through him. Whoever believes in him is not condemned, but whoever does not believe stands condemned already because they have not believed in the name of God's one and only Son" (John 3:15–18).

For those who repent of their sin and receive Jesus Christ as their Savior, the afterlife will consist of an eternity spent enjoying God. For those who reject Christ, however, the afterlife will be quite different. Jesus describes their destiny as "darkness, where there will be weeping and gnashing of teeth" (Matthew 8:12). As the heaven-sent authority on the afterlife, Jesus warns us to choose wisely: "Enter through the narrow gate. For wide is the gate and broad is the road that leads to destruction, and many enter through it. But small is the gate and narrow the road that leads to life, and only a few find it" (Matthew 7:13–14).

Speaking about life after death, G. B. Hardy, a Canadian scientist, once said, "I have only two questions to ask. One, has anyone ever defeated death? Two, did he make a way for me to do it also?"[1] The answer to both of Hardy's questions is yes. One person has both defeated death and provided a way for everyone who puts their trust in Him to overcome it as well. No one who trusts in Jesus Christ needs to fear death, but instead they can rejoice in the Lord's salvation:

> When the perishable has been clothed with the imperishable, and the mortal with immortality, then the saying that is written will come true: "Death has been swallowed up in victory."
>   "Where, O death, is your victory?
>   Where, O death, is your sting?"
>
>   1 Corinthians 15:54–55

20. Do unbelievers immediately go to hell when they die?

Of all the topics found in the pages of Scripture, none is so loathsome and dreadful as the subject of hell, yet we dare not be blinded by ignorance, repulsion, or unbelief, for hell is a frightening reality that ought not be dismissed on the grounds of fear or unpleasantness. Despite the objections of some, the flames of hell will not be extinguished by clever Scripture twisting or wishful thinking. The Bible has much to say about hell, and neither ignorance nor denial will cause this grim reality to go away.

We should understand the distinctions Scripture makes between Sheol and the eternal lake of fire. For purposes of this article, we will speak of "hell" as commonly understood: a place of torment after death. The Bible says that the unrepentant who die are immediately ushered into a dreadful holding place called Hades. In the following passage, Jesus details the horrid fate of an unregenerate sinner:

> There was a rich man who was clothed in purple and fine linen and who feasted sumptuously every day. And at his gate was laid a poor man named Lazarus, covered with sores, who desired to be fed with what fell from the rich man's table. Moreover, even the dogs came and licked his sores. The poor man died and was carried by the angels to Abraham's side. The rich man also died and was buried, and in Hades, being in torment, he lifted up his eyes and saw Abraham far off and Lazarus at his side. And he called out, "Father Abraham, have mercy on me, and send Lazarus to dip the end of his finger in water and cool my tongue, for I am in anguish in this flame." But Abraham said, "Child, remember that you in your lifetime received your good things, and Lazarus in like manner bad things; but now he is comforted here, and you are in anguish. And besides all this, between us and you a great chasm has been fixed, in order that those who would pass from here to you may not be able, and none may cross from there to us." And he said, "Then I beg you, father, to send him to my father's house—for I have five brothers—so that he may warn them, lest they also come into this place of torment." But Abraham said, "They have Moses and the Prophets; let them hear them." And he said, "No, father Abraham, but if someone goes to them from the dead, they will repent." He said to him, "If they do

not hear Moses and the Prophets, neither will they be convinced if someone should rise from the dead."

Luke 16:19–31 ESV

Hades (called "hell" in the King James Version) is described as a place of "torment" and "anguish" (Luke 16:23–24). The rich man went there immediately upon his death. Scripture's teaching is that all who die in their sins will immediately go to hell/Hades, where they will remain, conscious of their misery and despair, until summoned before God for judgment at the great white throne. These, who rejected God's mercy, must face His wrath, and they are eventually cast into the lake of fire (Revelation 20:11–15).

The lake of fire, the place of eternal punishment, was never intended for man; God ordained the lake of fire as the final stop for Satan and his army of fallen angels (Matthew 25:41; 2 Peter 2:4; Revelation 20:10). Regrettably, legions of unrepentant people will, by their own volition, spend eternity with Satan and the demons who joined his unholy rebellion (Matthew 10:28; 25:46). Those who choose hell are rebels to the very end.

God does not delight in the suffering of unredeemed man. He takes no pleasure in the death of the wicked and would rather see them turn from their evil ways and live (Ezekiel 33:11). Hell is a necessary reality. Imagine a man who spent his entire life avoiding God. Regarding the Scriptures as fanciful myths, he had no use for Bible reading. He considered prayer a one-sided conversation with a nonexistent being. He maligned sincere Christian believers with unsavory labels and mocked their adherence to biblical morality. From reaching the age of accountability until his dying breath, he distanced himself from his Creator. How, then, could such a man be happy in heaven? How could he tolerate the presence of Jesus Christ and His followers throughout the endless ages to come? For such a man, heaven would be a hell. It is God's will that none perish, but for those insistent rebels who reject His mercy, there is only justice. No third option exists.

Upon death, the lost are immediately sent to the place of their choosing, Hades (hell), where they will remain until the judgment convened at the close of our Lord's millennial kingdom. At that time, they will be consigned to the lake of fire along with Satan and his demonic forces. Forever, they will remain fixed in this diabolical state of being.

To think anyone would choose never-ending misery over God's everlasting joy is unfathomable, yet it is true.

21. Do believers immediately go to heaven when they die?

Yes, believers in Jesus Christ immediately go to heaven when they die. By "heaven," we mean a real place of comfort and blessedness where God dwells. Of course, the bodies of believers remain on earth, awaiting the resurrection, but their souls/spirits go to be with the Lord (see 2 Corinthians 5:8).

The biblical teaching that believers immediately go to heaven when they die differs from what some groups teach. According to the Watchtower Bible and Tract Society, faithful Jehovah's Witnesses who die remain in an unconscious state of "soul sleep" until the resurrection. At the resurrection, Jehovah "remembers" them, and they are brought back to life. The doctrine of soul sleep is also taught by Seventh-day Adventists. The Roman Catholic Church teaches that all believers, Catholic and non-Catholic, who die enter purgatory, a place of punishment to atone for the sins not covered by Jesus' sacrificial death on the cross. Once these sins have been sufficiently punished, the faithful, now purified, may enter paradise. Proponents of both views make seemingly good arguments in favor of their beliefs, but neither the doctrine of soul sleep nor the teaching of purgatory is biblical.

As our Lord Jesus suffered on the cross, another condemned prisoner sought forgiveness. Our Lord's response to the repentant thief's request refutes both the doctrine of soul sleep and the belief in purgatory:

> One of the criminals who were hanged railed at him, saying, "Are you not the Christ? Save yourself and us!" But the other rebuked him, saying, "Do you not fear God, since you are under the same sentence of condemnation? And we indeed justly, for we are receiving the due reward of our deeds; but this man has done nothing wrong." And he said, "Jesus, remember me when you come into your kingdom." And he said to him, "Truly, I say to you, today you will be with me in paradise."
>
> Luke 23:39–43 ESV

Jesus did not say, "After a determined time of misery and suffering, you will be with me in paradise"; neither did He say, "After an extended period of unconscious stupor, you will regain sentience and be with me in paradise." According to the promise of Jesus, the repentant thief would join his Savior in paradise that very day.

> So we are always of good courage. We know that while we are at home in the body we are away from the Lord, for we walk by faith, not by sight. Yes, we are of good courage, and we would rather be away from the body and at home with the Lord.
>
> 2 Corinthians 5:6–8 ESV

Here, the apostle Paul did not say that to be away from the body is to cease consciousness until the resurrection. He also did not say that to be out of the body was to be at home in purgatory.

In Jesus' story of the rich man and Lazarus, the beggar died, and "the angels carried him to Abraham's side" (Luke 16:22). This seems to have been an immediate event, with no lapse of time between Lazarus's death and his being picked up by the angels. In John's vision of heaven, he sees "under the altar the souls of those who had been slain because of the word of God and the testimony they had maintained" (Revelation 6:9). As these believers in heaven await vengeance and the resurrection of their bodies, they converse with the Lord. It seems that, as soon as they were martyred, they were in heaven.

At the death of a believer, his or her disembodied spirit immediately enters the joyful presence of our Lord Jesus. At the rapture, the saint's spirit joins his or her resurrected body—a glorified body impervious to the ravages of aging, illness, disease, suffering, and death (1 Corinthians 15:42–53). At the close of Jesus' millennial reign, heaven as it is passes away, and God unveils the New Jerusalem, our eternal home (Revelation 21:1–4). Our present mortal bodies are not fit for eternity, but our new bodies will never become ill, grow old, or die. We shall live gloriously with Him in perfect bodies throughout the endless ages of eternity.

With this end in mind, the apostle Paul broke out in joyous apostrophe: "'O death, where is your victory? O death, where is your sting?' The sting of death is sin, and the power of sin is the law. But thanks be to God, who gives us the victory through our Lord Jesus Christ" (1 Corinthians 15:55–57 ESV).

22. What happens after death?

Within the Christian faith, there is a significant amount of confusion regarding what happens after death. Some hold that after death everyone "sleeps" until the final judgment, after which everyone will be sent to heaven or hell. Others believe that at the moment of death, people are instantly judged and sent to their eternal destinations. Still others claim that, when people die, their souls/spirits are sent to a "temporary" heaven or hell to await the final resurrection, the final judgment, and the finality of their eternal destination. So, what exactly does the Bible say happens after death?

First, for the believer in Jesus Christ, the Bible tells us that after death believers' souls/spirits are taken to heaven, because their sins were forgiven when they received Christ as Savior (John 3:16, 18, 36). For believers, death means being "away from the body and at home with the Lord" (2 Corinthians 5:6–8; Philippians 1:23). However, passages such as 1 Corinthians 15:50–54 and 1 Thessalonians 4:13–17 describe believers being resurrected and given glorified bodies. If believers go to be with Christ immediately after death, what is the purpose of this resurrection? It seems that, while the souls/spirits of believers go to be with Christ immediately at death, the physical body remains in the grave "sleeping." At the resurrection of believers, the physical body is resurrected, glorified, and reunited with the soul/spirit. This reunited and glorified body-soul-spirit will be the state of existence for believers for eternity in the new heaven and new earth (Revelation 21–22).

Second, for those who do not receive Jesus Christ as Savior, death means everlasting punishment. However, similar to the destiny of believers, it seems that unbelievers also go to a temporary holding place to await their final resurrection, judgment, and eternal destiny. Luke 16:22–23 describes a rich man being tormented immediately after death. Revelation 20:11–15 describes all the unbelieving dead being resurrected, judged at the great white throne, and cast into the lake of fire. Unbelievers, then, are not sent to the final "hell" (the lake of fire) immediately after death; rather, they are sent to a temporary realm of fiery judgment and anguish. The rich man cried out, "I am in agony in this fire" (Luke 16:24).

After death, a person resides in either a place of comfort or a place of torment. These realms act as a temporary "heaven" and a temporary "hell" until the resurrection. At that point, the soul is reunited with the body, but no one's eternal destiny will change. The first resurrection is for the "blessed and holy" (Revelation 20:6)—everyone who is in Christ—and those who are part of the first resurrection will enter the millennial kingdom and, ultimately, the new heaven and new earth (Revelation 21:1). The other resurrection happens after Christ's millennial kingdom, and it involves a judgment on the wicked and unbelieving "according to what they had done" (Revelation 20:13). These, whose names are not in the book of life, will be sent to the lake of fire to experience the "second death" (Revelation 20:14–15). The new earth and the lake of fire—these two destinations are final and eternal. People go to one or the other, based entirely on whether they have trusted Jesus Christ for salvation (Matthew 25:46; John 3:36).

23. Where do you go when you die?

The Bible is absolutely clear that there are only two options for where you go when you die: heaven or hell. The Bible also teaches that you can determine where you go when you die. How? Read on.

First, the problem. We have all sinned (Romans 3:23). We have all done things that are wrong, evil, or immoral (Ecclesiastes 7:20). Our sin separates us from God, and, if left unresolved, our sin will result in our being eternally separated from God (Matthew 25:46; Romans 6:23). This eternal separation from God is hell, described in the Bible as an eternal lake of fire (Revelation 20:14–15).

Now, the solution. God became a human being in the person of Jesus Christ (John 1:1, 14; 8:58; 10:30). He lived a sinless life (1 Peter 2:22; 1 John 3:5) and willingly sacrificed His life on our behalf (1 Corinthians 15:3; 1 Peter 1:18–19). His death paid the penalty for our sins (2 Corinthians 5:21). God now offers us salvation and forgiveness as a gift (Romans 6:23) that we must receive by faith (John 3:16; Ephesians 2:8–9). "Believe in the Lord Jesus, and you will be saved" (Acts 16:31). Trust in Jesus as your Savior, relying on His sacrifice alone as the payment for your sins, and the Word of God promises you eternal life in heaven.

Where do you go when you die? It is up to you. God offers you the choice. God invites you to come to Him. It is your call.

If you feel God drawing you to faith in Christ (John 6:44), come to the Savior. If God is lifting the veil and removing your spiritual blindness (2 Corinthians 4:4), look to the Savior. If you are experiencing a spark of life in what has always been dead (Ephesians 2:1), come to life through the Savior.

Where do you go when you die? Heaven or hell. Through Jesus Christ, hell is avoidable. Receive Jesus Christ as your Savior, and heaven will be your eternal destination. Make any other decision, and eternal separation from God in hell will be the result (John 14:6; Acts 4:12).

If you understand the two possibilities of where you go when you die and you want to trust Jesus Christ as your Savior, it is time to call on God for salvation. As an act of faith, pray something like the following: "God, I know that I am a sinner, and I know that because of my sin I deserve to be eternally separated from you. Even though I do not deserve it, thank you for loving me and providing the sacrifice for my sins through the death and resurrection of Jesus Christ. I believe that Jesus died for my sins, and I trust in Him alone to save me. From this point forward, help me to live my life for you instead of for sin. Thank you, Jesus, for saving me!"

24. Do we become angels after we die?

Angels are beings created by God (Colossians 1:15–17) and are entirely different from humans. They are God's special agents to carry out His plan and to minister to the followers of Christ (Hebrews 1:13–14). There is no indication that angels were formerly humans or anything else—they were created as angels. Angels have no need of, and cannot experience, the redemption that Christ came to provide for the human race. First Peter 1:12 describes their desire to look into salvation, but it is not for them to experience. Had they been formerly humans, the concept of salvation would not be a mystery to them, having experienced it themselves.

Yes, they rejoice when a sinner turns to Christ (Luke 15:10), but salvation in Christ is not for them.

Eventually, the body of the believer in Christ will die. What happens then? The spirit of the believer goes to be with Christ (2 Corinthians 5:8). The believer does not become an angel. It is interesting that both Elijah and Moses were recognizable on the Mount of Transfiguration. They had not transformed into angels but appeared as themselves—although glorified—and were recognizable to Peter, James, and John (Matthew 17:1–3).

In 1 Thessalonians 4:13–18, Paul says that believers in Christ are asleep in Jesus; that is, their bodies are dead, but their spirits are alive. This text tells us that, when Christ returns, He will bring with Him those who are asleep in Him. Then their bodies will be raised, made new like Christ's resurrected body, to be joined with their spirits. All believers in Christ who are living at the return of Christ will have their bodies changed to be like Christ's body, and they will be completely new in their spirits, no longer having a sin nature.

All the believers in Christ will recognize one another and live with the Lord forever. We will serve Him throughout eternity, not as angels, but along with the angels. Thank the Lord for the living hope He provides for the believer in Jesus Christ.

25. Do babies and children go to heaven when they die?

The Bible doesn't explicitly answer the question of whether children who die before they are born again go to heaven. However, enough indirect information can be pieced together from Scripture to provide a satisfactory answer, which relates to infants as well as those with mental handicaps and others.

The Bible speaks to the fact that all of us born of human parents are born with an inherited corruption from Adam that ensures we will inevitably sin. This is often referred to as original sin. While God created Adam and Eve in His own likeness (Genesis 5:1), the Bible says that, once Adam and Eve fell and became sinful, Adam fathered children "in *his own* likeness" (Genesis 5:3, emphasis added; cf. Romans 5:12). All human beings have inherited a sinful nature through Adam's original act of disobedience; Adam became sinful, and he passed that sinfulness along to all his descendants.

The Bible speaks matter-of-factly about children who do not know enough "to reject the wrong and choose the right" (Isaiah 7:16). One reason people are guilty before God, Romans 1 says, is that they refuse to acknowledge what is "clearly seen" and "understood" concerning God (verse 20). People who, upon seeing and evaluating the evidence of nature, reject God are "without excuse." This raises some questions: If a child is too young to know right from wrong and possesses no capacity for reasoning about God, then is that child exempted from judgment? Will God hold babies responsible for not responding to the gospel, when they are incapable of understanding the message? We believe that granting saving grace to babies and young children, on the basis of the sufficiency of Christ's atonement, is consistent with God's love and mercy.

In John 9, Jesus heals a man born blind. After the physical healing, the man goes through a process of receiving his spiritual sight. At first, the man is ignorant; he knows Jesus' name but not where to find Him (John 9:11–12). Later, he arrives at the truth that Jesus is a prophet (verse 17) and that He is from God (verse 33). Then, in speaking to Jesus, the man admits his ignorance and his need for the Savior. Jesus asks him, "Do you believe in the Son of Man?" and the man replies, "Who is he, sir? . . . Tell me so that I may believe in him" (verses 35–36). Finally, having seen the light spiritually, he says, "Lord, I believe," and worships Jesus (verse 38).

Following the expression of faith from the man born blind, Jesus encounters some spiritually blind Pharisees: "Jesus said,

'For judgment I have come into this world, so that the blind will see and those who see will become blind.' Some Pharisees who were with him heard him say this and asked, 'What? Are we blind too?' Jesus said, 'If you were blind, you would not be guilty of sin; but now that you claim you can see, your guilt remains'" (John 9:39–41). In other words, Jesus says, "If you were truly ignorant [blind], you would have no guilt. It's because you are *not* ignorant—you are willfully unbelieving—that you stand guilty before God."

The principle Jesus lays down in John 9 is that God does not condemn people for things they are unable to do. "Sin is measured by the *capacities* or *ability* of people, and by their opportunities of knowing the truth. If people had no *ability* to do the will of God, they could incur no blame. If they have all proper *ability*, and no *disposition*, God holds them to be guilty."[2] According to this principle, babies and young children who are unable to accept or reject Christ are not held accountable for unbelief.

It would seem that, before people are mature enough to discern right from wrong (sometimes called reaching "the age of accountability"), they are not held responsible by God. Toddlers sin, and they bear Adam's corrupt nature. Yet, lacking the ability to understand the concept of right and wrong, they are under God's grace, in our opinion.

Other biblical anecdotes (e.g., David testifying that he would be reunited with his dead baby after death in 2 Samuel 12:23) support the reasonable belief that infants go to heaven when they die. The same holds true for those with mental disabilities who cannot comprehend right and wrong.

26. How is physical death related to spiritual death?

The Bible has a great deal to say about death and, more importantly, what happens after death. Physical death and spiritual death are both a separation of one thing from another. Physical death is the separation of the soul from the body, and spiritual death is the separation of the soul from God. When understood that way, the two concepts are closely related. Both physical death and spiritual death are included in the very first references to death.

In the creation account (Genesis 1–2), we read how God created a variety of living beings. These animals had life, an inward element that gave movement and energy to their physical bodies. Scientists are still at a loss to explain what truly causes life, but the Bible is clear that God gives life to all things (Genesis 1:11–28; 1 Timothy 6:13). The life that God gave to mankind was different from that which He gave to animals. In Genesis 2:7, God "breathed into [the man's] nostrils the breath of life, and the man became a living being." Whereas animals have a purely physical life, humans have both a physical and a spiritual element of life, and the death we experience likewise has both a physical and a spiritual element.

According to Genesis 2:17, God told Adam that, if he ate of the tree of the knowledge of good and evil, he would "certainly die." Some skeptics have tried to use this verse to show an inconsistency in the Bible because Adam and Eve did not die the very day they ate of that fruit. However, there are different types of life, and there are different types of death. A person can be physically alive and spiritually dead (Ephesians 2:1, 5) and vice versa (Matthew 22:32). When they sinned (Genesis 3:7), Adam and Eve immediately lost their spiritual life. They become "dead" to godliness, they forfeited Eden, and they came under God's judgment (eternal death). Their shame triggered a correlating action, as they hid from God (Genesis 3:8)—their internal separation from God manifested itself in an external separation from Him.

In addition to the immediate spiritual death they experienced, they also began the process of physical death, even though it took many years for death to have its full effect. The process of death can be seen in a bouquet of flowers. Flowers growing in a garden are plainly alive—they are connected to stems and roots and receive nourishment from their respective plants. When the flowers are separated from their life source, they still have the *appearance* of life and can maintain that appearance for several days, depending on the conditions. But, regardless of the care they are given, cut flowers are already dying, and that process cannot be reversed. The same is true for mankind cut off from God, their source of life.

The physical death that entered the world with Adam's sin (Romans 5:12) affected all living things. It is difficult for us to conceive of a world without death, but that is what Scripture teaches was the condition before the fall. All living things began the process of dying when sin entered the world. When physical death occurs, there is a definite separation of life from the body. When that separation occurs, there is nothing humans can do to reverse it. "The wages of sin is death" (Romans 6:23), and death comes upon everyone because everyone has sinned. Everyone is subject to physical death because of the presence of sin in this world, as well as his or her own personal sins. From a human perspective, physical death seems to be the ultimate punishment, but there are deeper levels of death to be considered.

The life that God breathed into Adam (Genesis 2:7) was more than just animal life; it was the breath of God, resulting in a being with a soul. Adam was created spiritually alive, connected to God in a special way. He enjoyed a relationship with God, but when he sinned, that relationship was broken. Spiritual death has implications both before and after physical death. Though Adam was still physically alive (but beginning the dying process), he became spiritually dead, separated from relationship with God. In this present life on earth, spiritual death brings great loss: We lose God's favor, the knowledge of God, and the desire for God.

Everyone begins life "dead in . . . transgressions and sins" (Ephesians 2:1), resulting in a life focused on sinful desires. Jesus taught that the only remedy for spiritual death is a spiritual rebirth (John 3:3–5) through faith in Him. This rebirth results in a reconnection to the source of life. Jesus pictured this in John 15.1–6.

He is the vine, and we are the branches. Without a connection to Him, we have no real life in us. When we have Jesus, we have life (cf. 1 John 5:11–12).

For those who refuse to accept God's salvation, physical death and spiritual death culminate in the "second death" (Revelation 20:14). This eternal death is not annihilation, as some have taught, but is a conscious, eternal punishment for sins in the lake of fire, where individuals are separated from the presence of the Lord (2 Thessalonians 1:9). Jesus spoke of this eternal separation from God in Matthew 25:41 and referenced the conscious torment of individuals in the story of the rich man and Lazarus (Luke 16:19–31).

God is not willing that any should perish but that all should come to repentance (2 Peter 3:9). We do not have to remain spiritually dead. To repent means to change one's mind and involves confessing sin to God and turning to Christ. Those who have received God's salvation have turned from death to life (1 John 3:14), and the second death has no power over them (Revelation 20:6).

27. What does it mean that the dead know nothing (Ecclesiastes 9:5)?

Ecclesiastes 9:5 reads, "For the living know that they will die, / but the dead know nothing; / they have no further reward, / and even their name is forgotten." This verse is sometimes used as a proof text for annihilationism, but that concept is not what is being communicated here. The "dead know nothing," but in what way?

It is clear from other places in the Bible that this verse cannot mean the dead have absolutely no knowledge. Jesus said in Matthew 25:46 that sinners "will go away to eternal punishment, but the righteous to eternal life." Every person will spend eternity with God in heaven or apart from Him in hell. It seems that each person will have feelings, thoughts, and abilities that exist in eternity.

In fact, Luke 16:19–31 offers an example of human capabilities in the afterlife. Lazarus is in paradise in eternal joy, while the rich man is in torment in hell (called "Hades"). The rich man has feelings, can talk, and has the ability to remember, think, and reason.

The key to understanding the statement "the dead know nothing" is found in the theme of the book of Ecclesiastes. Ecclesiastes is written specifically from an *earthly* perspective. The key phrase, repeated throughout the book, is *under the sun*, used about thirty times. Solomon is commenting on an earth-bound life, "under the sun," without God. His conclusion, also repeated throughout the book, is that everything from that perspective is "vanity" or "meaningless" (Ecclesiastes 1:2 KJV, NIV).

When a person dies "under the sun," the earthly perspective, without God, is that it's over. He is no longer under the sun. There is no more knowledge to give or be given, just a grave to mark his remains. Those who have died have "no further reward" in this life; they no longer have the ability to enjoy life like those who are living. Eventually, "even their name is forgotten" (Ecclesiastes 9:5).

Ecclesiastes 9:5 displays a chiastic structure (ABBA format) like this:

> *A* For the living know that they will die,
> *B* but the dead know nothing;
> *B* they have no further reward,
> *A* and even their name is forgotten.

Lines 1 and 4 are parallel thoughts in the sense that the living know death is coming while those who remain after a person dies quickly forget those who have died. The second and third lines lay down associated ideas in parallel; the dead know nothing, and the dead can no longer enjoy or be rewarded for their activities in this life.

The saying "the dead know nothing" seems to be a negative sentiment, but it is not without a positive message. Solomon encourages his readers to live life to its fullest, knowing life is short.

In the end, the fullest life is one that honors God and keeps His ways (Ecclesiastes 12:13–14).

28. Is it possible to be so heavenly minded that you are of no earthly good?

Oliver Wendell Holmes, Sr., is attributed with the quote "Some people are so heavenly minded that they are of no earthly good." The same sentiment found its way into a song by Johnny Cash: "You're shinin' your light yes and shine it you should / You're so heavenly minded and you're no earthly good."[3] The criticism that some Christians are "so heavenly minded that they are of no earthly good" is a catchy turn of phrase, but is it warranted?

The accusation that some Christians are too heavenly focused and therefore not paying enough attention to earthly matters is based on a false premise, namely, that love of God makes one less capable or less concerned with the practical affairs of the world. Being "heavenly minded" does not result in isolating oneself from the world, ignoring contemporary issues, or declining to be involved. Just the opposite: Being heavenly minded results in attempting to please God, who has given us work to do in this world.

Committed, heavenly minded Christians have always tackled the social, environmental, and political problems of the day. Some of the most impactful people in history have been Christians whose faith moved them to action. Devoted Christians such as John Newton and William Wilberforce worked tirelessly to abolish the slave trade in England. Christians such as missionary Amy Carmichael, philanthropist George Müeller, and journalist Robert Raikes rescued children in peril, founded orphanages, and established schools. History is full of Christians who positively impacted the world. Their motivation was not simply the need for social reform; rather, they were compelled to do what they did by their strong faith in Jesus and their heavenly focus. It is the very fact that Christians are "heavenly minded" that causes them to help others while spreading the life-changing truth of the gospel.

The Bible insists that Christians be focused on heavenly things: "So we fix our eyes not on what is seen, but on what is unseen, since what is seen is temporary, but what is unseen is eternal" (2 Corinthians 4:18). When Christians have their eyes set on Christ, they gain an eternal perspective, and they are of great "earthly good" as their faith impacts their lives and the lives of others (Colossians 3:2; Hebrews 12:1–3).

Scripture teaches that good deeds naturally follow when a person places faith in Jesus Christ (James 2:18). Christians serve the Lord and positively impact the world because of their hope of eternity with Him (1 Corinthians 15:58). True religion involves helping orphans and widows in their distress (James 1:27), doing to others as we would have them do to us (Luke 6:31), giving to those in need (Proverbs 19:17; Acts 20:35), dealing honestly in business (Leviticus 19:11), treating animals humanely (Proverbs 12:10), and proclaiming freedom to those who are enslaved by sin (Ephesians 1:7). A truly heavenly minded Christian is one who lives out his or her faith in service to the Savior and who wants to act justly, love mercy, and walk humbly with God (Micah 6:8).

It is the earthly minded who accomplish nothing of eternal value. People who are earthly minded are of the world and seek after its desires, which are not from God (1 John 2:15). Being earthly minded is short-sighted: "The world and its desires pass away, but whoever does the will of God lives forever" (1 John 2:17). Those who are focused on serving Christ and bringing Him glory will make a lasting impact on earth and for eternity (see Matthew 6:19–21).

29. Is _____ in heaven or hell?

Wondering if a certain person is in heaven or in hell is common, especially right after a celebrity or other famous figure passes away.

Many times, people also wonder about a deceased friend or relative. Did he or she go to heaven or hell? We should be careful when making assertions about a specific person's eternal destiny.

It's impossible to say for certain what relationship another person has (or had) with God. We cannot see the heart, but God can (1 Samuel 16:7). Neither do we possess the ability to peer into heaven or hell to see the residents there. Human beings simply aren't equipped to make infallible pronouncements on whether someone is in heaven or hell. For this reason, it's good to speculate less and focus more on a basic understanding of the gospel. What we know for sure is that there are only two destinations for the dead: heaven and hell. Those who have accepted Christ by faith will be with God after death. Those who have rejected Christ will be separated from God forever.

A better question than "is so-and-so in heaven or hell?" is "was so-and-so's life consistent with saving faith in Christ?" This allows for a more objective answer. Some lives clearly fall on one side or the other of that criterion. Yet, according to the Bible, it's possible to "put on a show" and still be lost (Matthew 7:21–23). And it's possible to struggle to apply one's faith and still be saved (Matthew 21:31). Only God truly knows what goes on in the heart, even when a person seems beyond hope.

Rather than make a definitive claim with respect to an individual's eternal destiny, our preference is to point to what the Bible says about those who trust in Christ and then allow others to form their own opinion. Realistically, the best we can do is say that someone who has passed away is "probably saved" or "probably not saved."

Those who publicly profess faith in Christ and whose lives seem consistent with that profession would be on the "probably saved" side of the spectrum. When a person's words and actions give evidence of faith in Christ, then it's reasonable to assume that he will be with God when he passes. This conclusion is tempered by the fact that externals are not what actually matter;

it's possible for pious behavior to mask a lost soul (Matthew 23:26–28).

Those who overtly reject Christ would be on the "probably unsaved" end of the scale. Those who make it clear by their words and actions that they reject the gospel give evidence they were not saved and will go to hell when they pass. At the same time, God can save anyone, no matter how close to death he or she is (Matthew 20:1–16; Luke 23:43). We don't know what may happen in the secrecy of a person's heart in the last moments before death. Further, there are those who may struggle with habitual sin despite having legitimate saving faith.

One's public persona, especially for celebrities, often differs from one's private life. This dichotomy can make it virtually impossible to say what a public figure's real views on faith and spirituality were. Even if we can make an educated guess, that assumption has to be kept in perspective.

Ultimately, the gospel is the only hope for any of us after this life. Regardless of whether some particular person is in heaven, our personal need for Christ remains. We can confidently say that in Christ there is salvation (John 6:27). If a person accepts the gospel and is born again, he or she will be with God after death. Our focus should be on our own spiritual needs and the needs of those still living.

SECTION 4

General Questions about Heaven

30. Is heaven real?

Heaven is indeed a real place. The Bible tells us that heaven is God's throne (Isaiah 66:1; Acts 7:48–49; Matthew 5:34–35). After Jesus' resurrection and appearance on earth to His disciples, He was taken up into heaven and sat at the right hand of God (Acts 1:9–11). "Christ did not enter a sanctuary made with human hands that was only a copy of the true one; he entered heaven itself, now to appear for us in God's presence" (Hebrews 9:24). Jesus not only went before us, entering heaven on our behalf, but He has a present ministry in heaven, serving as our high priest in the true tabernacle made by God (Hebrews 6:19–20; 8:1–2).

Jesus Himself said that there are many rooms in God's house and that He has gone before us to prepare a place for us. We have the assurance of His promise that He will one day come back to earth and take us to where He is in heaven (John 14:1–4). Our belief in an eternal home in heaven is based on an explicit promise of Jesus. Heaven is most definitely a real place.

When people deny the existence of heaven, they deny not only the written Word of God but also the innermost longings of their own hearts. Paul addressed this in his letter to the Corinthians, encouraging them to cling to the hope of heaven so that they would not lose heart. Although we "groan and sigh" in our earthly state (2 Corinthians 5:4 NLT), we have the hope of heaven always before us and are eager to get there. Paul urged the Corinthians to look forward to their eternal home in heaven, a perspective that would enable them to endure hardships and disappointments. "For our light and momentary troubles are achieving for us an eternal glory that far outweighs them all. So we fix our eyes not on what is seen, but on what is unseen, since what is seen is temporary, but what is unseen is eternal" (2 Corinthians 4:17–18).

Just as God has put in men's hearts the knowledge that He exists (Romans 1:19–20), so are we "programmed" to desire heaven. Heaven is the theme of countless books, songs, and works of art. Unfortunately, our sin has barred the way to heaven. Since heaven is the abode of a holy and perfect God, sin has no place there. Fortunately, God has provided for us the key to open the doors of heaven—salvation in Jesus Christ (John 14:6). All who believe in Him and seek forgiveness for sin will find the doors of heaven swung wide open for them.

May the future glory of our eternal home motivate us all to serve God faithfully and wholeheartedly: "My dear brothers and sisters, stand firm. Let nothing move you. Always give yourselves fully to the work of the Lord, because you know that your labor in the Lord is not in vain" (1 Corinthians 15:58).

31. Is heaven eternal?

Is heaven eternal? The answer seems obvious at first glance. We sing about spending eternity in heaven, and we say to the bereaved in consolation, "He is with God now." Many Christians believe that heaven and hell are the final destination for all humans, and that's correct if we use broad, generic definitions of the terms *heaven* and *hell*. Scripture provides more nuance. The "heaven" we preach about as the spiritual destination for believers is not our eternal abode. Instead, it serves as a place where deceased saints await the final unveiling of God's plan. So, although it is accurate to say that all who die in Christ currently reside in heaven, that is not the end of the journey.

In Scripture, the word *heaven* can describe the sky, outer space, and the dwelling place of God (Genesis 1:14–18; John 14:2; Ephesians 4:8). In the last usage, *heaven* has no physical description, but it is where all believers will go after death. Paul refers to it as the "third heaven" and describes "a man" being caught up there, likely recounting his own supernatural experience (2 Corinthians 12:1–9). The third heaven is also known as paradise.

Our eternal abode, however, is the new earth, which will come with a new heaven and is sometimes called the "eternal state." The old heaven and earth will be destroyed, as Peter writes in 2 Peter 3:10–13:

> But the day of the Lord will come like a thief. The heavens will disappear with a roar; the elements will be destroyed by fire, and the earth and everything done in it will be laid bare.
>
> Since everything will be destroyed in this way, what kind of people ought you to be? You ought to live holy and godly lives as you look forward to the day of God and speed its coming. That day will bring about the destruction of the heavens by fire, and the elements will melt in the heat. But in keeping with his promise we are looking forward to a new heaven and a new earth, where righteousness dwells.

The eternal state is the final piece in God's plan, where the earth will be restored to its original design, accompanied by the new heaven. It will be more than a mere consolation for the troubles in this fallen world; it will be a renewal, complete with the restoration of Eden (Revelation 22:1–4). Believers will receive new bodies and have access to the Holy City, the New Jerusalem, and the tree of life (1 Corinthians 15:42–44; Philippians 3:20–21; Revelation 21:1–2, 27; 22:2). The new earth can be envisioned as "Eden 2.0," the utopia humans have long desired, written about, and even depicted in movies. Our instinctual yearning for something more in life is right because we are made for eternity (Ecclesiastes 3:11). The current order of existence is temporary and subject to God's curse because of mankind's sin (Genesis 3:17–18; Romans 8:20–22).

The prospect of a new heaven and a new earth means that God has a reason for the current brokenness. Just as we cannot experience the beauty of healing without the pain of sickness, so perhaps can we not fully appreciate the joy of the new earth without experiencing this old one. As we await the return of Jesus, our blessed hope, we are confident "that the creation itself will be liberated from its bondage to decay and brought into the freedom and glory of the children of God" (Romans 8:21).

While it is accurate to say that believers will go to heaven after death, our final destination is a new, recreated earth. Far from playing harps on clouds for eternity, we will work without the strains of the curse, live without the struggles of sin and suffering, and have direct fellowship with God (Revelation 21:3). The new earth is reserved for redeemed humanity, as nothing evil can enter (Revelation 21:8, 27). As sinful humans, our only passage to this new world is through Christ.

32. How can heaven be perfect if all of our loved ones are not there?

The word *perfection* carries the idea of wholeness and a lack of nothing. If something is perfect, then it's complete. So, how can heaven be perfect if some people are missing? Wouldn't it be better if all our loved ones were there?

God is perfect (Psalm 18:30). God's dwelling place is perfect. God's plan of salvation is perfect. In God's plan (which is perfect), He extends the righteousness of Christ to all who trust in Him. What happens to those who do not trust in Christ? They are rejecting perfection, rejecting God's dwelling place, and rejecting God Himself. As John 3:18 says, "Whoever does not believe stands condemned already because they have not believed in the name of God's one and only Son." To force people to believe, to ignore their sin, or to bypass Christ would be to destroy the perfection of heaven.

When we arrive in heaven, our perspective will change. Our limited, earthly perspective will be replaced by a holy, heavenly perspective. Speaking of the eternal state, Revelation 21:4 says that God "will wipe every tear from their eyes. There will be no more death or mourning or crying or pain, for the old order of things has passed away." Missing our loved ones would presumably fall under the category of pain or mourning. Perhaps we will have no knowledge or remembrance of them at all. Perhaps we will have come to understand how our loved ones' absence glorifies God. "Now all we can see of God is like a cloudy picture in a mirror. Later we will see him face to face. We don't know everything, but then we will, just as God completely understands us" (1 Corinthians 13:12 CEV). In the meantime, we accept by faith that what God says about heaven is true and that we will experience perfection for eternity.

For a brief description of eternity, see Revelation 21–22. Everything is made new; everything is splendid, glorious, and blessed.

That will include us. Our bodies, souls, and spirits will be completely blessed. Sin will no longer be a factor, and our thoughts will be in agreement with God's (1 John 3:2). God has a plan to comfort His people (Isaiah 40:1), to perfect His redeemed (Hebrews 10:14), and to provide for them forever (Psalm 23:6).

Right now, our focus should not be on how we can enjoy heaven or the eternal state without all of our loved ones there; rather, we should focus on how we can, right now, point our loved ones to faith in Christ—so that they *will* be there.

33. Will Jesus still have the scars of crucifixion in heaven?

The Bible does not specifically tell us that Jesus, now in heaven, has retained the scars of His crucifixion. We can't be absolutely sure, but we believe He does still have the scars—the only scars anywhere in heaven—based on a few clues in Scripture.

When Jesus rose from the dead, His resurrected, glorified body still had the scars. He invited Thomas, who had doubted the resurrection, to see and feel the scars of crucifixion: "Put your finger here," Jesus said; "see my hands. Reach out your hand and put it into my side. Stop doubting and believe" (John 20:27). Jesus' scars were visible and touchable, post-resurrection.

John's description of Jesus in the first part of the book of Revelation does not mention any scars or wounds (Revelation 1:12–16). Of course, the description is quite symbolic, emphasizing Jesus' glory, power, and majesty. Later in the same book, Jesus is pictured as "a Lamb, looking as if it had been slain" (Revelation 5:6). This picture suggests scars, but, again, it is highly symbolic, and we are careful not to draw details of physical appearance from such a passage.

If Jesus still has the scars of crucifixion in heaven, why might He have chosen to retain them? The scars borne by our Savior represent several profoundly important things:

First, the scars are an eternal witness to the incarnation of the Son of God. A spirit can have no scars, but "the Word became flesh and made his dwelling among us" (John 1:14). Jesus received the scars while He walked this earth as one of us. Since His incarnation, Christ remains in the flesh forever. Just as the Son lost none of His divinity when He came to earth, so He lost none of His humanity when He returned to heaven. He is forever God in the flesh, the perfect (and only) Mediator between God and man (1 Timothy 2:5).

Second, the scars reveal why Jesus came to earth: to be a sacrifice for us. As Jesus said, "the Son of Man did not come to be served, but to serve, and to give his life as a ransom for many" (Matthew 20:28). He came to suffer for us, to save us from sin. He came to reconcile us to the Father in heaven. That reconciliation required His suffering:

> He was pierced for our transgressions,
>   he was crushed for our iniquities;
> the punishment that brought us peace was on him,
>   and by his wounds we are healed.
>
> Isaiah 53:5

Jesus' scars of crucifixion attest to His sacrifice.

Third, the scars reveal that God loved us while we were still sinners. The sin of mankind put Jesus on the cross. As He was being arrested, Jesus told His enemies, "This is your hour—when darkness reigns" (Luke 22:53). And the world itself grew dark when He was on the cross (Luke 23:44). But thus it had to be. If God had waited until we somehow made ourselves righteous, we would never have known salvation. We weren't interested in righteousness, and we could not attain to it even if we desired it (Romans 3:10–12). Evil scarred Jesus, and those scars are proof that "God demonstrates his own love for us in this: While we were still sinners, Christ died for us" (Romans 5:8).

Fourth, the scars Jesus still bears in heaven reveal that He suffered as we do in this world. He knows our pain. He wept with those who wept (John 11:35). He resisted against sin unto the point of bloodshed (Hebrews 12:4). He is our High Priest who empathizes with our weaknesses (Hebrews 4:15).

Fifth, the scars signify that death has been defeated. The wounds Jesus received were lethal, but He triumphed over the grave. What's more, He allows us to share in His triumph. The scars show that our final victory is in Him. "'Where, O death, is your victory? Where, O death, is your sting?' . . . But thanks be to God! He gives us the victory through our Lord Jesus Christ" (1 Corinthians 15:55, 57).

The scars of crucifixion Jesus will likely possess for eternity speak of the greatest love ever (John 15:13). Presumably, Jesus will have the only scars in heaven, in which case we will see a visible reminder of His praiseworthiness. Without the event that occasioned those scars, *no one else would be there.*

34. Will we remember our earthly lives when we are in heaven?

Isaiah 65:17 says, "See, I will create new heavens and a new earth. The former things will not be remembered, nor will they come to mind." Some interpret Isaiah 65:17 as saying that we will have no memory of our earthly lives in heaven. However, one verse earlier, in Isaiah 65:16, the Bible says, "For the past troubles will be forgotten and hidden from my eyes." It is likely only our "past troubles" will be forgotten, not all of our memories. Our memories will eventually be cleansed, redeemed, healed, and restored, not erased. There is no reason why we could not possess many memories from our earthly lives. The memories that will be cleansed are the ones that involve sin, pain, and sadness. Revelation 21:4 declares, "'He will wipe every tear from their eyes. There will be no more death' or mourning or crying or pain, for the old order of things has passed away."

The fact that the former things will not come to mind does not mean that our memories will be wiped clean. The prophecy could be suggesting the wondrous quality of our new environment. The new earth will be so spectacular, so mind-blowing, that everyone will quite forget the drudgery and sin of the current earth. A child who is scared of the shadows in his room at night completely forgets his nocturnal fear the next day on the playground. It's not that the memories have been wiped out, only that, in the sunshine, they don't come to mind.

Also, it's important to make a distinction between the eternal state and the current heaven. When a believer dies, he or she goes to heaven, but that is not our final destination. The Bible speaks of "a new heaven and a new earth" as our eternal, permanent home. Both Isaiah 65:17 and Revelation 21:1 refer to the eternal state, not the current heaven. The promise of wiping away every tear does not come until after the tribulation, after the final judgment, and after the re-creation of the universe.

In his apocalyptic vision, John sees sorrow in heaven: "I saw under the altar the souls of those who had been slain because of the word of God and the testimony they had maintained. They called out in a loud voice, 'How long, Sovereign Lord, holy and true, until you judge the inhabitants of the earth and avenge our blood?'" (Revelation 6:9–10). John is obviously in heaven (Revelation 4:1–2), and he sees and hears those who obviously remember the injustice done to them. Their loud calls for vengeance indicate that, in the current heaven, we will remember our lives on earth, including the bad things. The current heaven of Revelation 6 is temporary, though, giving way to the eternal state in Revelation 21.

The story of Lazarus and the rich man (Luke 16:19–31) is further proof that the dead remember their earthly lives. The rich man in Hades asks Abraham to send Lazarus back to earth to warn the rich man's brothers of the fate awaiting the unrighteous (verses 27–28). The rich man obviously remembers his relatives. He also remembers his own life of self-serving and sinful comfort (verse 25). The memories of the rich man in Sheol become part of his misery. The story does not mention Lazarus's memories, but Abraham has definite knowledge of goings-on on earth (verse 25). It's not until we reach the eternal state that the righteous will leave all sorrow behind.

35. Will we be able to see all three members of the Trinity in heaven?

Before considering if we will actually be able to see God the Father, the Son, and the Holy Spirit, we need to establish that they are three Persons. Without delving too deeply into the doctrine of the Trinity, we should understand that the Father is not the same Person as the Son, the Son is not the same Person as the Holy Spirit, and the Holy Spirit is not the same Person as the Father. Also, they are not three Gods. They are three distinct Persons, yet they are all the one God. Each has a will, can speak, can love, etc., and these are demonstrations of personhood. They are in absolute, perfect harmony and are of one substance. They are coeternal, coequal, and co-powerful. If any one of the three were removed, there would be no God.

So, in heaven, there are three Persons of the Godhead. But will we be able to *see* all three Persons? Revelation 4:3, 6 gives us a description of heaven and the throne that is occupied by God and by the Lamb: "The one who sat there had the appearance of jasper and ruby. A rainbow that shone like an emerald encircled the throne. . . . Also in front of the throne there was what looked like a sea of glass, clear as crystal." Since God dwells in "unapproachable light" and is one "whom no one has seen or can see" (1 Timothy 6:16), God is described in terms of the reflected brilliance of precious stones. First Corinthians 2:9 says, "No eye has seen, no ear has heard, and no mind has imagined what God has prepared for those who love him" (NLT). Because of God's holiness, it may be that we will never be able to look upon His face, but this is speculation.

Revelation 5:6 tells us that, in heaven, the Lamb stands in the center of the throne, and there are descriptions of Him clothed in brilliant white. Since the Lamb represents Christ Jesus, and we know that human eyes have beheld Him after His resurrection, it seems reasonable to conclude that, in heaven, we will be able to look upon Him.

The Holy Spirit, by the very nature of His being, is able to take various forms at will. When Jesus was baptized, the Holy Spirit descended on Him in the form of a dove (Matthew 3:13–17). At Pentecost, the Holy Spirit was accompanied by a loud rushing noise and was seen as tongues of fire (Acts 2:1–4). It may not be possible to see the Holy Spirit in heaven unless He chooses to manifest Himself in some form, but, again, that is speculation.

Mere mortals do not have the ability to grasp the wonders of heaven—it is entirely beyond our comprehension. Whatever heaven is like, it will far exceed our wildest imaginings! What we know is that we will be worshiping our great God as our hearts are filled with wonder that He died to save sinners.

36. Do pets/animals go to heaven? Do pets/animals have souls?

The Bible does not give any explicit teaching on whether animals have souls or whether our pets will be in heaven. However, we can use general biblical principles to develop some clarity on the subject. We might be able to form an educated guess.

The Bible states that both man (Genesis 2:7) and animals (Genesis 1:30; 6:17; 7:15, 22) have the "breath of life"; that is, both man and animals are living beings. The primary difference between human beings and animals is that humanity is made in the image and likeness of God (Genesis 1:26–27), but animals are not. Being made in the image and likeness of God means that human beings are like God in some ways: They have a mind, emotion, and will; they are capable of reason and creativity; and they have a spiritual part that continues after death. If animals, including our pets, do have a soul or spirit (an immaterial aspect), it must therefore be of a different and lesser quality. This difference possibly means that animal souls do not continue in existence after death.

God created the animals as part of His "very good" creation (Genesis 1:31). Later, when it came time to rid the world of mankind's wickedness through the global flood, God preserved the animal kingdom. They were important enough in God's plan to issue this command to Noah: "You are to bring into the ark two of all living creatures, male and female, to keep them alive with you" (Genesis 6:19). Of course, this doesn't mean that our pets are in heaven, but it does show that God cares about animals and that a world without animals is contrary to His plan.

All of creation, including the animals, was affected by mankind's fall and suffers because of our sin. But there is a promised restoration: "Against its will, all creation was subjected to God's curse. But with eager hope, the creation looks forward to the day when it will join God's children in glorious freedom from death and decay" (Romans 8:20–21 NLT). One day, God's creation will experience "freedom" and share in the glory of the children of God. Does this mean that animals who have died will be resurrected? Possibly, but the passage does not explicitly say that.

There will definitely be animals on earth during the millennial kingdom. Wolves, leopards, goats, cows, lions, bears, cobras, and vipers are all mentioned (Isaiah 11:6–8). No matter how dangerous some of those animals may be in today's world, in the millennium, "they will neither harm nor destroy on all my holy mountain" (Isaiah 11:9; cf. 65:25). There is no reason why there could not be pets or animals on the new earth, too (Revelation 21:1).

It is impossible to say whether some of the animals mentioned as part of the kingdom might be the pets we had here on earth. We do know that God is just and that, when we get to heaven, we will find ourselves in complete agreement with His decision on this issue, whatever it may be.

37. Do we receive mansions in heaven?

The night before Jesus was crucified, He told His disciples that He would be leaving them and that they could not go with Him (John 13:33). Peter asked where He was going and why they couldn't go with Him, and Jesus assured them that they would follow Him eventually (John 13:36–37). Jesus said, "My Father's house has many rooms; if that were not so, would I have told you that I am going there to prepare a place for you? And if I go and prepare a place for you, I will come back and take you to be with me that you also may be where I am" (John 14:2–3).

This saying of Jesus has confused many because of the King James Version's use of the word *mansions*. In the KJV, John 14:2 says, "In my Father's house are many mansions." The picture conjured by many who read this is based on common ideas of "mansions" in this world. Poems are written and songs are sung about our "mansion just over the hilltop." But does heaven consist of large, imposing estates dominated by opulent residences? Do each of us really get our own Monticello, Montpelier, or even greater manse? Such an idea is unwarranted, based on John 14:2.

Jesus was not describing physical characteristics of heaven. He was assuring His disciples that they would have a place—a permanent place—in God's abode. The Greek word translated "house" means "an abode," literally or figuratively, and, by implication, "a family." The word translated "mansions" (KJV) or "rooms" (NIV) means literally "abiding (not transitory) dwelling places for individuals." So, putting the Greek words together, Jesus is saying that in God's home (heaven) there will be many people in the family of God all abiding together. In God's heavenly household, believers will live in the presence of the Lord as a welcome part of His family. This is quite different from the vision of row upon splendid row of ornate mansions with manicured lawns.

The Lord assures us that He is preparing a place in heaven for His own, those who have come to Him in faith. In the meantime, the Holy Spirit prepares the redeemed on earth for their place in heaven. One day, all those bought with the blood of the Lamb will be part of "a great multitude that no one could count," all standing before the throne (Revelation 7:9). Here, again, the imagery is of multitudes of people together, not individuals living separately in personalized mansions.

38. How can we store up treasures in heaven?

Jesus told us to "store up for yourselves treasures in heaven" (Matthew 6:20). He linked this command to the desire of our hearts: "Where your treasure is, there your heart will be also" (Matthew 6:21; see also verses 10–20).

The Bible mentions rewards that await the believer who serves the Lord faithfully in this world (Matthew 10:41). A "great" reward is promised to those who are persecuted for Jesus' sake (Luke 6:22–23). Various crowns are mentioned (in 2 Timothy 4:8, e.g.). Jesus says that He will bring rewards with Him when He returns (Revelation 22:12).

We are to treasure the Lord Jesus most of all. When Jesus is our treasure, we will commit our resources—our money, our time, our talents—to His work in this world. Our motivation for what we do is important (1 Corinthians 10:31). Paul encourages servants that God has an eternal reward for those who are motivated to serve Christ: "Whatever you do, work at it with all your heart, as working for the Lord, not for human masters, since you know that you will receive an inheritance from the Lord as a reward. It is the Lord Christ you are serving" (Colossians 3:23–24).

When we live sacrificially for Jesus' sake or serve Him by serving the body of Christ, we store up treasure in heaven. Even seemingly small acts of service do not go unnoticed by God. "If anyone gives even a cup of cold water to one of these little ones who is my disciple, truly I tell you, that person will certainly not lose their reward" (Matthew 10:42).

Everyone, but especially those with more visible gifts such as teaching, singing, or playing a musical instrument, might be tempted to use their gift for their own glory. Another temptation they face is finding their identity in others' acknowledgment of their gift. Those who use their talents or spiritual gifts while coveting the praise of men rather than seeking God's glory receive their "payment" in full here and now. The applause of men was the extent of the Pharisees' reward (Matthew 6:16). Why should we work for worldly plaudits, however, when we can have so much more in heaven?

The Lord will be faithful to reward us for the service we give Him (Hebrews 6:10). Our ministries may differ, but the Lord we serve is the same. "The one who plants and the one who waters have one purpose, and they will each be rewarded according to their own labor" (1 Corinthians 3:8).

The rich young man loved his money more than God, a fact that Jesus incisively pointed out (Matthew 19:16–30). The issue wasn't that the young man was rich but that he "treasured" his riches and did not "treasure" what he could have in Christ. Jesus told the man to sell his possessions and give to the poor, "and you will have treasure in heaven. Then come, follow me" (verse 21). The young man left Jesus sad, because he was very rich. He chose this world's treasure and so did not lay up treasure in heaven. He was unwilling to make Jesus his treasure. The young man was religious, but Jesus exposed his heart of greed.

We are warned not to lose our full reward by following after false teachers (2 John 1:8). It is important to be like the Bereans, who "examined the Scriptures every day" to check what Paul was teaching (Acts 17:11). In studying God's Word, we can know the truth and better recognize falsehood.

The treasures that await the child of God will far outweigh any trouble, inconvenience, or persecution we may face (Romans 8:18). We can serve the Lord wholeheartedly, knowing that God is the One keeping score, and His reward will be abundantly gracious. "Always give yourselves fully to the work of the Lord, because you know that your labor in the Lord is not in vain" (1 Corinthians 15:58).

SECTION 5

Questions about What Heaven Will Be Like

39. What is heaven like?

Heaven is a real place described in the Bible. The word *heaven* is found 276 times in the New Testament alone. Scripture refers to three heavens. The apostle Paul was "caught up to the third heaven," but he was prohibited from revealing what he experienced there (2 Corinthians 12:1–9).

Since a third heaven exists, there must also be two other heavens. The first is most frequently referred to in the Old Testament as the "sky" or the "firmament." This is the heaven where weather happens, clouds float, winds whirl, and birds fly. The second heaven is what we call outer space, the region of the stars, planets, and other celestial objects (Genesis 1:14–18).

The third heaven, the location of which is not revealed, is the dwelling place of God. Jesus promised to prepare a place for His followers in heaven (John 14:2). Heaven is also the destination of Old Testament saints who died trusting God's promise of the Redeemer (Psalm 16:11; 23:6; 73:24–25). Whoever believes in Christ shall never perish but have eternal life (John 3:16).

The apostle John was privileged to see and report on the heavenly city, the New Jerusalem (Revelation 21:10–27). John witnessed that the new earth will possess the "glory of God" (Revelation 21:11), and the very presence of God will be among men. In the eternal state, there will be no night, and the Lord Himself will be the light of the city. The sun and moon will no longer be needed (Revelation 22:5).

The New Jerusalem will be filled with the brilliance of costly stones and crystal-clear jasper. The city has twelve gates (Revelation 21:12) and twelve foundations (Revelation 21:14). Paradise is restored: The river of the water of life flows freely, and the tree of life is available once again, yielding fruit monthly with leaves that heal the nations (Revelation 22:1–2). The Bible gives us a glimpse of heaven, but the reality of that place is beyond the ability of finite man to imagine (see 1 Corinthians 2:9).

Heaven is a place of "no mores." There will be no more tears, no more pain, and no more sorrow (Revelation 21:4). There will be no more separation, because death will be conquered (Revelation 20:6). The best thing about heaven will be the presence of our Lord and Savior (1 John 3:2). We will be face to face with the Lamb of God, who loved us and gave Himself for us. Because of His sacrifice, we can enjoy His presence for eternity.

40. Where is heaven?

Heaven is most certainly a real place. The Bible speaks of heaven's existence—and access to heaven through faith in Jesus Christ—but there are no verses that give us a geographical (or astronomical) location. The short answer to the question of "where is heaven?" is "heaven is where God is."

The place people call "heaven" is also referred to as "the third heaven" and "paradise" in 2 Corinthians 12:1–4. In that passage, the apostle Paul tells of a living man who was "caught up" to heaven and was unable to describe it. The Greek word translated "caught up" is also used in 1 Thessalonians 4:17 in describing the rapture, wherein believers will be caught up to be with the Lord.

Other verses indicating heaven to be "above" the earth are numerous. In Genesis 11:7, God says, "Come, let us go down" to see the tower of Babel. When the chariot of fire came to get Elijah, it took him "up to heaven" (2 Kings 2:11). Heaven is described as "high . . . above the earth" in Psalm 103:11 and the place from which the Lord "looks down" in Psalm 14:2. When Jesus prayed a prayer of thanksgiving, He did so "looking up to heaven" (Mark 6:41). In Acts 1:9–11 Jesus is taken "up" into heaven, and when God takes John to heaven in Revelation 4:1, He says, "Come up here." Such passages lead to the conclusion that heaven is "up" from our perspective; it is above us in an exalted position.

However, as J. I. Packer points out, "Since God is spirit, 'heaven' . . . cannot signify a place remote from us which he inhabits. The Greek gods were thought of as spending most of their time far away from earth in the celestial equivalent of the Bahamas, but the God of the Bible is not like this. Granted, the 'heaven' where saints and angels dwell has to be thought of as a sort of locality, because saints and angels, as God's creatures, exist in space and time; but when the Creator is said to be 'in heaven' the thought is that he exists on a different *plane* from us, rather than in a different *place*. That God in heaven is always near to his children on earth is something which the Bible takes for granted."[4]

Examples of God being near to us, even though He is in heaven, include the psalmist's assurance that "the LORD is close to the brokenhearted" (Psalm 34:18) and Paul's teaching that "he is not far from any one of us" (Acts 17:27). Moses asked the children of Israel, "What other nation is so great as to have their gods near them the way the LORD our God is near us whenever we pray to him?" (Deuteronomy 4:7). Heaven is only a prayer away.

The New Testament mentions heaven with considerable frequency, yet even then, details of its location are missing. We will never find heaven with telescopes, star charts, or deep space probes. We will only find heaven through faith in Jesus Christ.

More important than knowing where heaven is, is knowing the God of heaven, for the same reason that it's better to know your neighbor than the details of his house. On the night before His crucifixion, Jesus told His disciples, "You know the way to the place where I am going" (John 14:4). Thomas immediately raised an objection: "Lord, we don't know where you are going, so how can we know the way?" (verse 5). And Jesus answered, "I am the way and the truth and the life. No one comes to the Father except through me" (verse 6). We may not know the exact location of heaven, but we know the Way, for He is Jesus.

41. How big is heaven?

The word for "heaven" in the Old Testament is the Hebrew word *shameh* or *shamayim*, which refers to the sky, the lofty arch above the world where clouds move, and beyond that the place where the planets and stars exist. In the New Testament, the word *heaven* is a translation of the Greek *ouranos*, which means "the sky" and "the abode of God" and, by extension, "an eternal realm of happiness and glory." The sky in its vastness is a metaphor for the vastness and loftiness of God. It is the best earthly representation of the place where God lives.

How big is heaven—how big is the place where God lives? We know that God Himself is infinite. Heaven and earth cannot contain Him. In terms of time, there is no beginning or end to His years (Psalm 102:27); in terms of His kingdom, His reign will have no end (Luke 1:33); in terms of His character, He is unchanging (Hebrews 1:12; James 1:17). "God created the heavens and the earth" (Genesis 1:1). Of God's creation of the stars, Isaiah says, "Lift up your eyes and look to the heavens: Who created all these? He who brings out the starry host one by one and calls forth each of them by name. Because of his great power and mighty strength, not one of them is missing" (Isaiah 40:26).

Scientists have not even been able to chart the size of the known physical universe. There is a photo called the XDF (eXtreme Deep Field) that was put together from images taken by the Hubble Space Telescope over the course of ten years. That image shows a vast number of galaxies, each comprising billions of stars like our sun. Our sun is 93 million miles away from the earth. And the galaxies are very, very far apart—Andromeda, the closest galaxy to our own, is 2.2 million light years away. To give an idea of how far that is, a shuttle traveling at 18,000 miles per hour would need 37,200 years to travel *one* light year. The universe is absolutely huge—and God created it all.

So, how big is heaven? We don't know exactly. The Bible doesn't give any linear measurements. When John had his vision of heaven, he wrote, "There before me was a great multitude that no one could count, from every nation, tribe, people and language, standing before the throne and before the Lamb" (Revelation 7:9). Heaven is at least big enough for the innumerable multitude—and we can assume that there will be no crowding in heaven.

42. Are there different levels of heaven?

The closest thing Scripture says to there being different levels of heaven is found in 2 Corinthians 12:2: "I know a man in Christ who fourteen years ago was caught up to the third heaven. Whether it was in the body or out of the body I do not know—God knows."

Some interpret this as indicating that there are three different levels of heaven: a level for "super-committed Christians" or Christians who have obtained a high level of spirituality, a level for "ordinary" Christians, and a level for Christians who did not serve God faithfully. This view has no basis in Scripture.

Paul is not saying that there are three heavens or even three levels of heaven. In many ancient cultures, people used the term *heaven* to describe three different "realms"—the sky, outer space, and then a spiritual heaven. Paul was saying that God took him to the "spiritual" heaven—the realm beyond the physical universe where God dwells. The concept of different levels of heaven may have come in part from Dante's *The Divine Comedy* in which the poet describes both heaven and hell as having nine different levels. *The Divine Comedy*, however, is a fictional work. The idea of different levels of heaven is foreign to Scripture.

Scripture does speak of different rewards in heaven. Jesus said regarding rewards, "Look, I am coming soon! My reward is with me, and I will give to each person according to what they have done" (Revelation 22:12). Since Jesus will be distributing rewards on the basis of what we have done, we can safely say that there will be a time of reward for believers and that the rewards will differ somewhat from person to person.

Only those works that survive God's refining fire have eternal value and will be worthy of reward. Those valuable works are referred to as "gold, silver, costly stones" (1 Corinthians 3:12) and are those things that are built upon the foundation of faith in Christ. Those works that will not be rewarded are called "wood, hay or straw"; these are not evil deeds but shallow activities with no eternal value. Rewards will be distributed at the "judgment seat of Christ" (2 Corinthians 5:10), a place where believers' lives will be evaluated for the purpose of rewards. "Judgment" of believers never refers to punishment for sin. Jesus Christ was punished for our sin when He died on the cross, and God has said about us, "I will forgive their wickedness and will remember their sins no more" (Hebrews 8:12). What a glorious thought! The Christian need never fear punishment but can look forward to crowns of reward that he can cast at the feet of the Savior. In conclusion, there are not different levels of heaven, but there are different levels of reward in heaven.

43. Will there literally be streets of gold in heaven (Revelation 21:21)?

Heaven's streets of gold are often referenced in song and poetry, but they're harder to find in the Bible. In fact, there is only one passage of Scripture that mentions streets of gold, and that refers to the Holy City, the New Jerusalem: "The great street of the city was of gold, as pure as transparent glass" (Revelation 21:21). Earlier, John had described the whole city as being "of pure gold, as pure as glass" (verse 18). Do these verses tell us that the streets (and the city) will be literally made of gold in heaven? If so, what is the significance of having literal streets of gold?

The Greek word translated "gold" in Revelation 21:21 is *chrusion*, which can mean "gold, gold jewelry, or overlay." To translate it as "gold" makes perfect sense. Interpretative difficulties arise when attempting to determine which parts of the Bible to take literally and which parts to take figuratively. A good rule of thumb when studying the Bible is to take everything literally, unless it doesn't make sense to do so. In this passage there's no reason the gold must be figurative. John isn't just throwing out random descriptive terms; his mention of a "gold" street seems meant to be taken literally.

Earlier in Revelation 21, John is given a rod to measure out the city (verse 15), and he records precise measurements. Then he says, "The wall was made of jasper" (verse 18) and describes the city as composed of pure gold (verse 18). The foundations of the city walls are garnished with many specific precious stones and jewels (verses 19–20). The gates are made of pearl, and the main street is made of gold (verse 21). Everything in the description is specific as to composition, and there are no similes used—the street is not said to be "*like* gold," but "*of* gold."

So, if heaven's streets are made of gold, what is the point? Why is this an important detail? First, the gold is *valuable*. The streets of gold in the New Jerusalem indicate the worth of that place. In this world, we walk on gravel or pavement or asphalt. There, we will tread gold as if it were a commonplace building material. Everything in the New Jerusalem will be proportionately finer, richer, and more precious than anything we can imagine here.

Second, the gold is *beautiful*. The streets of gold and the whole city will gleam with an unmatched luster. Twice, John compares the purity of the gold in heaven to glass: The street is "as pure as transparent glass" (Revelation 21:21), and the city is "as pure as glass" (Revelation 21:18). Commentator Albert Barnes takes this to mean "that the golden city would be so bright and burnished that it would seem to be glass reflecting the sunbeams. . . . It is certain that, as nothing could be more magnificent, so nothing could more beautifully combine the two ideas referred to here— that of '*gold* and *glass*.'"[5]

Third, the gold is *transparent*. According to Revelation 21:21, the gold comprising the streets in heaven is "clear as crystal" (CEV) or "like transparent glass" (NET). This quality would set heavenly gold apart from earthly gold, to be sure. In our understanding, *transparent* cannot be a descriptor of gold. But heaven (the new earth) will be a place beyond our understanding. "Excellencies will be combined in the heavenly city which now seem incompatible."[6]

Fourth, the gold is *pure*. Everything about the new earth is pure, as God is pure. "The words of the LORD are flawless, . . . like gold refined seven times" (Psalm 12:6). The streets of gold in heaven reflect the pure light of God's blazing glory. And God's ability to purify is not confined to gold; God has purified all who will enter heaven through the blood of Jesus Christ. "If we confess our sins, he is faithful and just and will forgive us our sins and purify us from all unrighteousness" (1 John 1:9). Not only is God's holy city pure by His design, but so are the citizens of that city.

Fifth, the gold will *last*. The streets of gold in heaven denote the solidity and eternality of the new earth. The new earth will be a place of freedom from all sin and corruption (see Isaiah 35:8 and Revelation 21:27). Nothing will tarnish, rust, or grow dim. Everything and everyone will be forever flawless and absolutely impeccable.

Of course, there are some good teachers and scholars who do not hold to the idea of literal golden streets in heaven. It is a detail open to debate. However, taking the text at face value within the context of the whole chapter, there seems to be no reason to doubt the gold is literal.

Our focus in the New Jerusalem will not be the streets of gold. Perspectives will change, and what we treasure here will be trod underfoot in heaven. We may amass gold on earth, but one day we will see it as nothing more than paving material. Heaven will be a beautiful place, but nothing will ever be more beautiful or of greater value than the God who loves us and died to save us.

44. Will we experience time in heaven?

Benjamin Franklin reminded us that time is "the Stuff Life is made of."[7] Our earthly existence is marked by time. We "waste" it and "spend" it and "save" it; we have "time on our hands," or we "make up for lost time"; we speak of those who have "all the time in the world," while others are "running out of time"; and, then, "when our time is up," we exit this world. What about in heaven? Will we still experience time as we do now? The short answer is we really don't know.

First, let's be clear that, when we say "heaven," we are referring to the dwelling place of God. Revelation 21:3–4 says, "Look! God's dwelling place is now among the people, and he will dwell with them. They will be his people, and God himself will be with them and be their God. 'He will wipe every tear from their eyes. There will be no more death' or mourning or crying or pain, for the old order of things has passed away.'" The chapter goes on to describe the New Jerusalem, where believers will dwell for eternity.

Some argue that we will not experience time in heaven because "the city does not need the sun or the moon to shine on it, for the glory of God gives it light, and the Lamb is its lamp" (Revelation 21:23; see also Revelation 22:5). If the cycle of day and night is done away with, perhaps that signals the end of time—or at least our *measurement* of time. Also, we know that God exists apart from time (2 Peter 3:8), so perhaps those dwelling with Him will also be outside of time.

Others point to what seem to be clear references to experiencing time in heaven. For instance, Revelation 8:1 says, "There was silence in heaven for about half an hour." Was the "half an hour" simply John's measurement of the period of silence from an earthbound perspective, or did the residents of heaven also realize the passage of time?

Those in heaven appear to be aware of the passage of time on earth, and they may even describe it as "long." Revelation 6:9–10 says, "I saw under the altar the souls of those who had been slain because of the word of God and the testimony they had maintained. They called out in a loud voice, 'How long, Sovereign Lord, holy and true, until you judge the inhabitants of the earth and avenge our blood?'" Without a doubt, *how long* is a time-related phrase. These examples occur prior to the eternal state, but they may support the idea that time factors into our existence in the dwelling place of God.

Revelation 22:1–2, 5 speaks of the New Jerusalem: "Then the angel showed me the river of the water of life, as clear as crystal, flowing from the throne of God and of the Lamb down the middle of the great street of the city. On each side of the river stood the tree of life, bearing twelve crops of fruit, yielding its fruit every month. And the leaves of the tree are for the healing of the nations. . . . There will be no more night. They will not need the light of a lamp or the light of the sun, for the Lord God will give them light. And they will reign for ever and ever." The mention of "every month" and "for ever and ever" indicates the passage of time. One might suggest that John was only able to explain his vision in time-bound terms and that his words do not exactly represent the reality of the vision. However, *month* is still a time-related word.

When God created the world, He created time—there was a "beginning" (Genesis 1:1). He called the creation, including the reality of time, "very good" (Genesis 1:31). It seems, then, that time is something good and well-suited for God's creation. As part of God's creation, we are subject to time. Will that change in eternity? We cannot be sure.

Heaven is beyond our understanding. But we can rest in the fact that our God is good and what He has prepared for us is good. "He who was seated on the throne said, 'I am making everything new!' Then he said, 'Write this down, for these words are trustworthy and true.' He said to me: 'It is done. I am the Alpha and the Omega, the Beginning and the End. To the thirsty I will give water without cost from the spring of the water of life. Those who are victorious will inherit all this, and I will be their God and they will be my children'" (Revelation 21:5–7).

45. Will we have free will in heaven?

The fact that Adam and Eve had a choice to make in the Garden of Eden shows beyond all doubt that mankind was created with a free will. The first couple chose to sin, and that choice plunged the entire world into spiritual darkness, leading to our need of salvation. Through it all, mankind has retained his free will, and we will retain free will in heaven. Is it possible that people in heaven can exercise their free will to sin again and get kicked out of heaven? No, it is not possible.

To back up a bit, we need an acceptable definition of *free will*. We have free will, but not in the way most people think. Our freedom consists in the fact that we are free to choose according to our desires. As long as we have a minimum of two available options, we must make a choice, and we will always do so according to our strongest desire. But, in the case of a fallen sinner, he or she is not at liberty to choose according to righteousness. This is what Jesus means when He says that the one who sins "is a slave to sin" (John 8:34). This is not the language of "free will" as people typically think of it. The unregenerate person has a sinful nature; he is not just inclined to sin but driven by sinful impulses. It is perhaps helpful to say, "We are free to choose what we *want* but not free to want what we *ought*." This greatly limits our "freedom" because the list of things we want (as sinners) coincides with whatever pleases our sinful impulses. Our choices are for things that will ultimately destroy us (Proverbs 14:12). As Paul says, "Oh, what a miserable person I am! Who will free me from this life that is dominated by sin and death?" (Romans 7:24 NLT).

When we are saved, we are liberated from our natural bondage to sin. The Holy Spirit sovereignly regenerates us and in grace gives us the ability to want what we ought to want, namely, forgiveness, salvation, and honoring the lordship of Christ. When we trust in Jesus for salvation, we begin a moral progression, a journey toward holiness in which we put to death daily the sinful impulses that reside within us and strive toward godliness. In heaven we will be completely devoid of sin; our only desires will be for the things of God—things that bless us, fulfill us, and give us life. This is true liberty (see Romans 8:21). We will retain our free will in heaven, but our will is sanctified there. The sin nature will be gone.

In heaven we are completely conformed to the image of Christ (Romans 8:28–30). Our sanctification will be finished; we will not even *want* to sin. Also, in heaven there is no temptation to lure us and no devil to deceive us. Unlike Adam and Eve, we will face no test; our moral state will be secure. No one will get kicked out of heaven. Just as our Lord Jesus has a truly free will yet is without sin, so will we retain a free will yet be without sin. We will be like Him (1 John 3:2).

Before salvation, our free will on earth is limited by our inability to choose what is right. After salvation, our free will struggles between choosing what is right and what is wrong. In heaven our free will is limited by our inability to choose what is wrong. Our glorified state will allow us to exercise our free will in choosing what is true, noble, right, pure, lovely, and admirable (see Philippians 4:8).

46. Will it be possible for us to sin in heaven?

The Bible describes "heaven" or, more properly, the eternal state in Revelation chapters 21–22. Nowhere in those chapters is the possibility of sin mentioned. In fact, we have the promise that, in the eternal state, we will never experience death, sorrow, crying, or pain (Revelation 21:4)—the absence of those things is proof positive that sin is also absent, since all those things are the product of sin (see Romans 6:23).

The sinful will not be in heaven but in the lake of fire (Revelation 21:8). Nothing impure will ever enter heaven (Revelation 21:27). Outside of heaven are the unrepentant sinners (Revelation 22:15). An Old Testament prophecy also assures us that the kingdom of God will exclude sinfulness:

> A highway will be there;
>   it will be called the Way of Holiness;
>   it will be for those who walk on that Way.

The unclean will not journey on it;
    wicked fools will not go about on it. . . .
But only the redeemed will walk there.

Isaiah 35:8–9

So, the answer is, no, it will not be possible for us to sin in heaven.

God wills our sanctification (1 Thessalonians 4:3); that is, He wants to make us holy and free of sin. Our sanctification has three phases: positional sanctification, which saves us from the penalty of sin at the moment of faith in Christ; progressive sanctification, which saves us from the power of sin as we grow in Christ; and complete sanctification, which saves us from the presence of sin as we enter the presence of Christ. "When Christ appears, we shall be like him, for we shall see him as he is" (1 John 3:2). In other words, the process by which God sanctifies us involves justification, maturation, and glorification.

The glorification that God promises His children (Romans 8:30) necessarily includes sinlessness, because sinful beings cannot be glorious. Heaven, the place of God's glory, is sinless. Paul prays in 1 Thessalonians 5:23, "May the God of peace himself sanctify you completely" (esv), and he links the glorious appearing of Christ to our personal glorification: "When Christ, who is your life, appears, then you also will appear with him in glory" (Colossians 3:4). This glorified state will be our ultimate separation from sin, a total sanctification in every regard. It will not be possible for us to sin in heaven.

James 1:14 provides another assurance that we will not sin in heaven: "Each person is tempted when they are dragged away by their own evil desire and enticed." In this sinful world, we face temptation daily, and James identifies two forces that prompt us to sin: our own evil desire (our sin nature) and enticement (the devil's schemes). Neither of those forces will be in heaven. Our sin nature will have been eradicated in our glorification, and the tempter will have been consigned to the lake of fire, where he can do us no harm (Revelation 20:10).

The Bible's teaching is that heaven or the eternal state is completely holy. There will be no possibility of sin, we will be clothed with righteousness (Revelation 19:8), and we will be eternally confirmed in our state of bliss. The work that God promised to complete in us will have been finished (Philippians 1:6). Our deliverance will be complete, as the elect are redeemed—body, soul, and mind—to the glory of the Lamb (Revelation 5:6–10).

47. What will we do in heaven?

The stereotypical image of people in heaven floating on clouds strumming harps the livelong day is a gross and cartoonish misrepresentation of reality. The Bible presents heaven as a place of activity and movement. Yes, in heaven we will enjoy comfort (Luke 16:25) and rest from our labor (Revelation 14:13). But we will also be engaged in tasks that truly fulfill all that we were created to do. In heaven, we will finally be all that God created us to be.

Enjoy God's home

In Luke 23:43, Jesus turned to one of the thieves who was dying next to Him and declared, "Truly I tell you, today you will be with me in paradise." The word for "paradise" here is *paradeisō,* which means "a park, i.e. (specially), an Eden (place of future happiness, 'paradise')."[8] Jesus said, "Today you shall be with me *en tō paradeisō*" (not "*en nephele,*" which is Greek for "in clouds"). The point is that Jesus used the word for "a park." In context, the reference has to be to "the paradise of God" or "the park of God" (see Revelation 2:7). If parks and gardens in this world can be such beautiful and refreshing places, how much more beautiful will be the eternal Garden of God? How much more will it refresh the soul? Jesus promised the repentant thief they would be together in a pleasant place of happiness, peace, and rest.

Give an account

All believers will one day stand before the judgment seat of Christ, at which point we will give an account of ourselves and our faithfulness to the Lord (Romans 14:10–12). This will not be a time of judgment in the sense of condemnation for sin—all condemnation was taken away by Christ (Romans 8:1). But it will be a time of receiving rewards (or not receiving them) based on individual service to God. Each believer will "receive what is due . . . for the things done while in the body, whether good or bad" (2 Corinthians 5:10).

Worship and serve

Jesus taught us to "worship the Lord your God, and serve him only" (Matthew 4:10). We are commanded to worship God on earth, and we see worship taking place in heaven (Revelation 7:11). We are commanded to serve the Lord in this world, and we see people serving the Lord in the world to come: "The throne of God and of the Lamb will be in the city, and his servants will serve him" (Revelation 22:3). So, those are two things we'll be doing in heaven: worshiping and serving the Lord.

We are unable to fully serve God in this life due to sin, but in heaven "no longer will there be a curse upon anything" (Revelation 22:3 NLT). With the curse lifted, we will know true effectiveness in our service to God. Our worship will be pure. Our only motivation will be our love for God.

Learn and grow

In Christ "are hidden all the treasures of wisdom and knowledge" (Colossians 2:3). God is infinite, "the High and Lofty One Who inhabits eternity" (Isaiah 57:15 NKJV). How long will it take us to search out all the hidden treasures of wisdom? When will we be able to finally understand infinity? God is bigger than forever. At what point will we finally "grasp how wide and long and high and deep is the love of Christ, and . . . know this love that surpasses knowledge" (Ephesians 3:18–19)? We can keep learning all through eternity and never plumb the depths of God's glory. His ways are "unsearchable" and "inscrutable" (Romans 11:33 ESV). We will never stop learning about Him.

Fellowship with others

God's Word says we won't be in His paradise alone. We will be part of "a great multitude that no one could count" (Revelation 7:9). We will be sharing eternity with believing friends, family, and heroes of old. There will be no secrets there and nothing to hide as we fellowship with "the spirits of the righteous made perfect" (Hebrews 12:23). No wonder heaven will be a place of never-ending learning. Just getting to know everyone will take forever!

The Bible only provides glimpses of heaven. Whatever else we will be doing in God's eternal "park," we know it will be wonderful beyond our imagination. "No eye has seen, no ear has heard, and no mind has imagined what God has prepared for those who love him" (1 Corinthians 2:9 NLT).

48. Will we work/have jobs in heaven?

Heaven is a place where believers "will rest from their labor" (Revelation 14:13), but many are surprised to learn that heaven, or the eternal state, will also be a place where we will work. We will have tasks to perform. In the New Jerusalem, the Lamb is on the throne, and "his servants will serve him" (Revelation 22:3). The idea of heaven being a place where we lounge on clouds, benignly strumming harp strings, does not come from the Bible.

The thought of working in heaven may be distasteful to some, especially to those who have spent their lives in drudgery. But the "work" in heaven will be quite unlike our accustomed work in this world. Our job in eternity will simply be to serve the Lord. And we will be in a perfect environment.

From the beginning, God intended work to be part of the human experience. Work was His design; even before the fall, Adam had a job, as God placed him in the garden "to work it and take care of it" (Genesis 2:15). The woman was to assist with the work, as God created Eve to be Adam's "helper" (Genesis 2:20). Before the fall, the work God gave Adam and Eve was fulfilling, invigorating, and provided a sense of purpose. Only after the introduction of sin into the world did man's job become difficult (Genesis 3:17–19). So, while work is good, the "painful toil" we experience today is a result of living in a fallen world.

Even in our sinful world, work is honorable and still has the capacity to provide purpose and fulfillment. The problem is that many things can get in the way of enjoying a job: interpersonal problems, mismanagement, unrealistic demands, physical or mental fatigue, etc. In contrast, work in heaven will be pleasant and satisfying. There will be no interpersonal conflicts, impractical expectations, or fatigue, and we'll have the perfect Manager. As Randy Alcorn states in his book *Heaven*, "We'll also have work to do, satisfying and enriching work that we can't wait to get back to, work that'll never be drudgery."[9]

Another reason we believe that we will work in heaven is that God describes Himself as a worker. When asked by the Pharisees why He was, in their opinion, violating the Sabbath, Jesus replied, "My Father is always at his work to this very day, and I too am working" (John 5:17). The idea of God's children working in heaven should come as no surprise, since the Lord Himself works, and "we shall be like him, for we shall see him as he is" (1 John 3:2).

Believers will have jobs in heaven, just as the angels have special jobs that they carry out in worship and adoration. Angels are "servants" who do God's bidding (Hebrews 1:7). The angel who spoke to John called himself "a fellow servant with you" (Revelation 22:9). There are no unemployed angels in heaven, and there will be no unemployed saints.

In our current world, we have this command: "Whatever you do, work at it with all your heart, as working for the Lord" (Colossians 3:23). The work that Christians perform in heaven will have the same goal: to be an act of worship glorifying the Lord. The difference will be that, in eternity, the work that God has prepared for us will be instantly rewarding, constantly refreshing, and perfectly suited for who we were created to be.

49. Will we be able to see and know our friends and family members in heaven?

Many people say that the first thing they want to do when they arrive in heaven is see all their friends and loved ones who have passed on before them. That will indeed be a blessed time as believers reunite to fellowship, worship God, and enjoy the glorious wonders of heaven. One of the blessings is that we will know our friends and family members in heaven, and we will be known.

Our ability to recognize people in the afterlife is suggested in several passages of Scripture. At the transfiguration of Christ, Moses and Elijah made an appearance, and they were recognizable (Matthew 17:3–4). Though they had departed this world centuries prior, both Moses and Elijah remained distinct persons who had not lost their identity. In Luke 16:19–31, Abraham, Lazarus, and the rich man are all recognizable after death. King Saul recognized Samuel's description given by the witch of Endor when she summoned Samuel from the realm of the dead (1 Samuel 28:8–17). And, when David's young son died, David declared, "I will go to him, but he will not return to me" (2 Samuel 12:23). David's words imply that he believed he would recognize his son in heaven. In all these examples, the Bible seems to indicate that, after death, we will still be recognizable to each other.

The Bible declares that, when we arrive in heaven, we will "be like him [Jesus], for we shall see him as he is" (1 John 3:2). Just as our earthly bodies were of the first man, Adam, so will our resurrection bodies be like Christ's glorious body (1 Corinthians 15:47; Philippians 3:21). "And just as we have borne the image of the earthly man, so shall we bear the image of the heavenly man. . . . For the perishable must clothe itself with the imperishable, and the mortal with immortality" (1 Corinthians 15:49, 53). Jesus was recognizable after His resurrection (John 20:16, 20; 21:12; 1 Corinthians 15:4–7), so it stands to reason that we also will be recognizable in our glorified bodies.

Being able to see our loved ones is a glorious aspect of heaven. What a pleasure it will be to reunite with our loved ones and worship God with them in His presence for all eternity!

SECTION 6
Questions about What We Will Be Like in Heaven

50. What will we look like in heaven?

First Corinthians 15 addresses the resurrection and the resurrected body. Our heavenly bodies will be different from our natural bodies, with some stark contrasts. Our earthly bodies are subject to decay and corruption, but at the resurrection our bodies will be incorruptible: "The perishable must clothe itself with the imperishable" (1 Corinthians 15:53a). Likewise, our earthly bodies are characterized by mortality, being susceptible to death, but our resurrected bodies will be characterized by immortality and not susceptible to death (verse 53b). Also, whereas our natural bodies are prone to weakness, our resurrected bodies will be characterized by strength (verse 43).

We will have a body in heaven, and it will be the same body we have now. God redeems the *whole* person, body, soul, and spirit. But our resurrected body will be "heavenly" (1 Corinthians 15:40), "imperishable" (verse 42), glorified (verse 43), "spiritual" (verse 44), immortal (verse 53), and bearing Christ's image (verse 49). So, a lot will change, but we will not lose our identity. You will still be you.

Philippians 3:21 contains the promise that Jesus "will transform our lowly bodies so that they will be like his glorious body." After His resurrection, Jesus was recognizable for who He was (except when God prevented people from seeing, as in Luke 24:16). He had His hands and His feet (Luke 24:39). He ate food (Luke 24:42). His body was transformed, but it was still His body. The same will hold true for us in the resurrection.

Our natural bodies are associated with the word *dishonor* in 1 Corinthians 15:43 because they sustain damage; they scab and scar, they lose function, and eventually they decay and die. In short, they bear the marks of sin. Sometimes our bodies are damaged due to our own personal sin. Other times our bodies are marred by the sins of others. But everyone grows old, and the ravishes of time have their effect. The process of physical deterioration is a direct result of humanity's fall into sin. But God, through Christ's transforming power, is able to raise up His children with new, glorious bodies. When Jesus healed the man with the shriveled hand, "his hand was completely restored" (Luke 6:10). That's a small picture of what the resurrection of the body will accomplish. We will be "completely restored," completely free from the devastation of sin and possessing the glory of Christ instead.

The Bible does not say exactly what we will look like in heaven. What age we will appear to be? Will the texture of our hair stay the same? Will we have the same eye color? The same fingerprints? We can't answer any of these questions. We do know that whatever was associated with our natural, perishable condition will be removed. No more pimples, pains, or palsies. No more cataracts, coughs, or cancers. No more missing teeth, lazy eyes, or hereditary defects. Jesus may still bear His scars in heaven, but ours will be gone.

51. How does the Bible describe the glorified bodies we will possess in heaven?

While the Bible doesn't describe in detail the glorified bodies we will receive in heaven, we know that they will be like that of Jesus' resurrected body. Our mortal human bodies are described in 1 Corinthians 15:42–53 as perishable, dishonorable, and weak, all due to sin. Our immortal glorified bodies will be imperishable, honorable, and powerful. Our new bodies will no longer be "natural" bodies, subject to decay and death; we will live in "victory over sin and death," won by Christ on our behalf (1 Corinthians 15:57 NLT).

Being imperishable, our glorified bodies will no longer suffer from sickness and death, nor will they ever be subject to heat and cold or hunger and thirst. Our new bodies will be honorable in that they will not be shamed or shameful because of sin. When Adam and Eve sinned, the first thing they felt was shame because of their nakedness (Genesis 3:6–7). The Bible doesn't portray glorified bodies as being naked, but rather clothed in white garments (Revelation 3:4–5, 18). They will be pure and undefiled, with no taint of sin. Our earthly bodies are "weak" in many ways. Not only are we subject to the natural laws of gravity and time/space, but we are weakened by sin and its temptations. Our glorified bodies will be empowered by the Spirit who owns us, and weakness will be no more.

Just as our earthly bodies are perfectly suited to life on earth, our resurrected bodies will be suited for life in eternity. We will not be disembodied spirits but will have form and solidity (Luke 24:39–40). We will likely be able to enjoy food but will not be driven to it by necessity or fleshly desire (Luke 24:41–43). And like Moses and Elijah, we will bask in the glory of our Maker in the fellowship of His dear Son (Matthew 17:2–3; Philippians 3:10). Our resurrected, glorified bodies will be more like what God originally intended, rather than what we now abide in. Gone will be the infirmity and weakness of our sinful flesh; in their place will be eternal health and perpetual vitality. We will be glorified with Christ, and that glory will extend to the bodies we will inhabit.

52. What age will everyone be in heaven?

The Bible does not specifically answer this question. Will babies and children who die still be babies and children in heaven? What about elderly people who die—do they remain elderly in heaven? Some have guessed that, at the resurrection, babies are given a body that is "fast-forwarded" to the "ideal age," and those who die at an old age will have a body that is "rewound" to the prime of life. If this is what happens, then no one in heaven will appear as a child awaiting development, and no one will appear as a centenarian.

If everyone in heaven appears to be the same age, and that age is "ideal," then what is that ideal age? Again, the answer is not in the Bible. Some assume it to be around 30 years old. Some guess 33 since that is approximately the age Jesus was when He died. But those guesses are based on life as we currently know it. What about Moses who, at 120 years old, was still full of vim and vigor: "His eyes were not weak nor his strength gone" (Deuteronomy 34:7)? What about Methusaleh, who lived 969 years? Maybe in heaven he will look like he did when he was 500 years old, and none the worse for wear.

We all imagine that heaven will be a place where we will be forever young. What that "youth" will look like is anyone's guess. It's probably pointless to assign a numerical value to our apparent "age" in heaven. It's enough to know that God has a plan to transform us: "Dear friends, now we are children of God, and what we will be has not yet been made known. But we know that when Christ appears, we shall be like him, for we shall see him as he is" (1 John 3:2).

Whatever age we appear to be in heaven, we will be made perfect. We will be sinless, and our bodies will be remade flawless. Does that mean we will have no wrinkles in the skin? No age spots? No gray hair? We'll have to wait and see. We know that all traces of human fallenness will be gone, and we will finally be everything God intended us to be, to the praise of His glory.

53. Will there be such a thing as gender in heaven?

Some people believe that, in heaven, all people will be genderless; others believe that we will retain our gender in heaven and that the resurrection of the body will not change one's sex. Males will be males in heaven, and females will be females.

Those who promote the genderless view sometimes use Matthew 22:30 as a proof text. In that verse, Jesus speaks of people after the resurrection not participating in marriage—they become "like the angels." Jesus does say that people will not *marry* in heaven; however, He says nothing about *gender* in heaven.

Another passage cited by the supporters of the genderless view is Galatians 3:28: "There is neither Jew nor Gentile, neither slave nor free, *nor is there male and female,* for you are all one in Christ Jesus" (emphasis added). Some say that this verse presents the reality of the new creation: In Christ, who makes all things new, gender will be literally removed. In reply, we would say that Galatians 3:28 speaks of a spiritual unity in which neither men nor women have any special advantages or disadvantages in salvation. Heaven does not show favors on account of gender.

If there is no such thing as gender in heaven, then why did God create Adam and Eve as gendered beings? Some say that God knew gender would be necessary in a fallen world—that procreation would be needed to make up for the losses incurred by death. In the new earth, death will be abolished, thus making procreation (and gender) unnecessary. This explanation, however, is based on inference and assumption rather than anything explicit in the text of Scripture.

In fact, there is nothing in the Bible that indicates people will lose or change their gender in heaven. On the contrary, the Bible implies that we will remain who we are in heaven, and gender is part of who we are. Gender is part of our very nature and affects the way we relate to each other and to God. In paradise, Lazarus was still Lazurus, and Abraham was still Abraham (Luke 16:22–24). Elijah and Moses appeared in glory as themselves (Matthew 17:3). And the post-resurrection Jesus was still a "he" (see Luke 24:27). In each of these cases, the men are still men. No one lost his gender in heaven.

Augustine correctly saw the eternal state as a restoration and renewal of God's work, not an eradication of it. Augustine had "no doubt that both sexes shall rise. For there shall be no lust, which is now the cause of confusion. For before they sinned, the man and the woman were naked, and were not ashamed. From those bodies, then, vice shall be withdrawn, while nature shall be preserved. And the sex of woman is not a vice, but nature. . . . He, then, who created both sexes will restore both."[10]

In the eternal state, "there shall be no more curse" (Revelation 22:3 NKJV). So, the curse of sin is done away with. But gender was never part of the curse. God created humanity "male and female" (Genesis 1:27) before the fall. Gender, therefore, was part of the "very good" creation (Genesis 1:31). Life in heaven will be much different than it is now, but there is no reason to think that gender will be lost in heaven.

54. Will there be tears in heaven?

The Bible never specifically mentions tears in heaven. Jesus speaks of the rejoicing that takes place in heaven when one sinner repents (Luke 15:7, 10). The Bible says that, even now, those who believe in Jesus Christ "are filled with an inexpressible and glorious joy" (1 Peter 1:8)—if our earthly lives are so characterized by joy, what must heaven be like? Surely, heaven will be a much more joyful place. By contrast, Jesus described hell as a place of weeping and "gnashing of teeth" (Luke 13:28). So, after a cursory look at Scripture, it seems that tears will be a part of hell's domain, and heaven will be tear-free.

The promise of God has always been to take away the sorrow of His people and replace it with joy. "Weeping may stay for the night, but rejoicing comes in the morning" (Psalm 30:5). And "those who sow with tears will reap with songs of joy" (Psalm 126:5). As in all else, Jesus is our model in this. Our Lord is "the pioneer and perfecter of faith. For the joy set before him he endured the cross, scorning its shame, and sat down at the right hand of the throne of God" (Hebrews 12:2). Jesus' weeping gave way to awaiting joy.

There is coming a time when God will remove all tears from His redeemed ones. "He will swallow up death forever. The Sovereign LORD will wipe away the tears from all faces; he will remove his people's disgrace from all the earth. The LORD has spoken" (Isaiah 25:8). The apostle John quotes Isaiah's prophecy as he records his vision of heaven in Revelation 7:17. At the very end of time, God fulfills His promise: "He will wipe every tear from their eyes" (Revelation 21:4). What's interesting is the timing of this event: it happens after the great white throne judgment (Revelation 20:11–15) and after the creation of the new heaven and new earth (Revelation 21:1).

Consider this: if God wipes away every tear *after* the new creation, that means that tears could still be possible up to that point. It is conceivable, though by no means sure, that there are tears in heaven leading up to the new creation. Tears in heaven would seem out of place, but here are a few times when tears might fall, even in heaven:

1) *At the judgment seat of Christ.* Believers will face a time when "the quality of each person's work" will be tested (1 Corinthians 3:13). He whose works are found to be "wood, hay or straw . . . will suffer loss but yet will be saved—even though only as one escaping through the flames" (verses 12 and 15). Suffering the loss of a reward will certainly be a sad time—could it be a time of tears in heaven, as we realize how much more we could have honored the Lord? Perhaps.

2) *During the tribulation.* After the fifth seal is broken, the persecution of believers during the tribulation intensifies. Many are slain by the beast or Antichrist. These martyrs are pictured in Revelation 6 as being under the altar in heaven, waiting for the Lord to enact vengeance: "They called out in a loud voice, 'How long, Sovereign Lord, holy and true, until you judge the inhabitants of the earth and avenge our blood?'" (verse 10). These souls are in heaven, but they still remember the occasion of their death and they seek justice. Could these individuals be shedding tears as they keep vigil? Perhaps.

3) *At the eternal doom of loved ones.* Assuming that people in heaven have some knowledge of what happens on earth, it might be possible that we will know when a loved one rejects Christ and passes into a godless eternity. This would be a distressing knowledge, naturally. During the great white throne judgment, will those in heaven be able to see the proceedings, and, if so, will they shed tears over those who are damned? Perhaps.

We have been speculating. There is no biblical mention of tears in heaven. Heaven will be a place of comfort, rest, fellowship, glory, praise, and joy. If there are tears, for the reasons listed above, they will all be wiped away in the eternal state. "Comfort, comfort my people, says your God" (Isaiah 40:1). And "he who was seated on the throne said, 'I am making everything new!'" (Revelation 21:5).

55. Will we sleep in heaven?

Sleep is a physical necessity for our earthly bodies. Without sleep, our brains stop working correctly, and our bodies refuse to cooperate. The sleep-wake cycle is just another of the many cycles God has put into place on the earth—others include the cycle of the changing seasons, day and night, and the water cycle. These cycles are part of life on this planet. However, after death, we will be in a different realm. Upon death, those who are "in Christ" will be immediately with Him (2 Corinthians 5:8) but will not yet have their completely restored bodies. We must wait for the resurrection to receive those (1 Corinthians 15:40; 2 Corinthians 4:14; John 5:28–29). Most likely, in the interim, after death and before the resurrection, our souls will not need sleep; rather, we will enjoy unbroken worship and joy in the presence of the Lord.

"Sleeping" in heaven—the spiritual realm where we await the resurrection—may not even be possible or necessary. Jesus described the temporary resting place for the righteous as being near Abraham (Luke 16:23). We will have some type of body, and we will recognize each other (Luke 16:22–24). We might have some knowledge of the affairs on earth (Luke 16:27–28; Revelation 6:9–10). But we should take careful note of the reactions of human beings who saw God in His glory as did Isaiah (Isaiah 6:1–5), Moses (Exodus 33:20–23), and John (Revelation 1:17). Living in the manifest presence of the Lord God Almighty will change everything. The things of earth, including sleep, will no longer have the same value to us.

However, God created human beings to inhabit a physical realm. He intends to restore all things (Acts 3:21). At the resurrection our spirits, which have been with Christ, will be reunited with our restored bodies. We will then inhabit the new, completely restored earth with Jesus (Isaiah 65:17; Revelation 21:1–2). Eternity will be spent living in perfect bodies on a perfect earth with Jesus as our undisputed King. In the eternal state, sleep may again be part of our experience, as could eating and drinking (Luke 14:15; Revelation 19:9). But sleep will not be necessary due to exhaustion or weakness because our bodies will be perfect like Jesus' body after His resurrection (Luke 24:41–42).

The fact is that we don't know enough from Scripture to state definitively whether we will sleep in heaven, in the millennium, or in the eternal state. That's one of the thousands of questions we will have answered in heaven. One thing is for sure: When we first see Jesus, sleep will be the last thing on our minds.

56. Will we eat food in heaven?

Many people ask whether we will eat food in heaven because eating is not only necessary but also so very enjoyable! Many people conclude that what is enjoyable on earth (sex, family relationships, etc.) will naturally be present in heaven. While we will definitely have the fulfillment of all enjoyment in heaven, it will be because we are in the presence of the Lord. Whatever we enjoy in heaven won't be there because we enjoyed it on earth but because it finds its fulfillment in God. The Bible does not give us a detailed answer to the question of eating food in heaven, but a few observations from the Scriptures are in order.

When the Lord Jesus celebrated the Passover with His disciples shortly before His crucifixion, He referred to eating and drinking in the kingdom: "Truly I tell you, I will not drink again from the fruit of the vine until that day when I drink it new in the kingdom of God" (Mark 14:25). The earthly millennial kingdom is certainly in view here, and in that kingdom many will have already received their resurrection bodies. It would appear from this statement that we, in our glorified bodies, will eat and drink in the millennial kingdom. Jesus ate food post-resurrection (Luke 24:42), so it stands to reason that we will, too. But what about eating food in the heavenly kingdom?

When John had his vision of the New Jerusalem, he saw "a pure river of water of life, clear as crystal, proceeding from the throne of God and of the Lamb. In the middle of its street, and on either side of the river, was the tree of life, which bore twelve fruits, each tree yielding its fruit every month. The leaves of the tree were for the healing of the nations. And there shall be no more curse" (Revelation 22:1–3 NKJV). This text does not say whether we will actually eat the fruit of the tree of life.

Eating from the tree of life *is* mentioned in Jesus' message to the Ephesian church in Revelation 2:7. The Lord makes this promise: "To the one who is victorious, I will give the right to eat from the tree of life, which is in the paradise of God." If we are to take this literally, the tree of life will grow in the heavenly kingdom, it will bear fruit, and we will eat of that fruit.

So, we might eat food in heaven, but we cannot know for sure what the menu may contain. It has been suggested that our diet will be like that of Adam and Eve in paradise before the fall: "God said, 'I give you every seed-bearing plant on the face of the whole earth and every tree that has fruit with seed in it. They will be yours for food'" (Genesis 1:29).

In the end, we don't really know if, or what, we will eat in heaven. Believers only "know in part" (1 Corinthians 13:9). The joy of being forever with the Bread of Life is beyond our ability to comprehend, for "what we will be has not yet been made known. But we know that when Christ appears, we shall be like him, for we shall see him as he is" (1 John 3:2).

57. Will we be naked in heaven?

The idea that we will be naked in heaven is based on a comparison between the original creation in Genesis and the new creation in Revelation. Some believe, based on these two sections of Scripture, that people will be naked in heaven.

Adam and Eve were naked in the Garden of Eden before the fall (Genesis 2:25). It was only after they sinned that they felt a need to cover their bodies (Genesis 3:7), and God provided clothing for them after He pronounced curses (Genesis 3:21). From then on in Scripture, nakedness is almost always associated with sexual sin and/or shame. But, when God creates the new heaven and new earth, He will abolish the curse (Revelation 22:3). Since clothing came with the curse, some speculate that the removal of the curse will allow for the removal of clothing. So, in eternity, they conclude, we will be naked.

Of course, there is nothing inherently sinful about the human body. And there would be nothing wrong with glorified believers in heaven being naked. There will be no lust in heaven, and no shame—no sin of any kind. But biblical descriptions of heavenly beings often include a mention of some type of clothing. It does not seem to be the case that believers will spend eternity naked.

Angelic beings are described in the Bible as wearing some kind of garments. In Daniel's vision, the messenger (either an angelic being or a pre-incarnate appearance of Christ) was "dressed in linen clothing, with a belt of pure gold around his waist" (Daniel 10:5 NLT). Similarly, the angel guarding Jesus' tomb was wearing garments: "His appearance was like lightning, and his clothes were white as snow" (Matthew 28:3).

The redeemed in heaven are also described as clothed. In Revelation 4:4, the twenty-four elders around the throne of God wear white clothing and have golden crowns. Revelation 3:5 says that those who belong to Christ will be "dressed in white" in heaven. The Bible never hints that anyone in heaven is unclothed.

In our opinion, we will not be naked in heaven. Yes, Adam and Eve were naked before they sinned, but their nakedness was indicative of innocence and sinlessness. Unlike Adam and Eve, we have never been in a state of innocence, so, when we get to heaven, we are pictured as being covered by the "clothing" provided by the sacrifice of Christ (see Revelation 3:18).

58. Will there be marriage in heaven?

Jesus said, "At the resurrection people will neither marry nor be given in marriage; they will be like the angels in heaven" (Matthew 22:30). This statement clearly answers the question of whether there will be marriage in heaven. The answer is no.

The Sadducees had approached Jesus with a hypothetical situation: Suppose a woman had been married multiple times (seven times, in fact). "At the resurrection," they posed, "whose wife will she be of the seven, since all of them were married to her?" (Matthew 22:28). It was a "gotcha" question, because the Sadducees did not even believe in the resurrection (verse 23). Jesus rebuked them for their lack of knowledge of the Scriptures and their discounting of the power of God (verse 29). And He plainly said there will be no marriage in heaven (verse 30). In that regard, people in heaven will be like the angels, who likewise do not marry.

The fact that there will be no marriage in heaven does not mean that a husband and wife will no longer know each other in heaven. It also does not mean that a husband and wife could not still have a close relationship in heaven. What it does seem to indicate, though, is that a husband and wife will no longer be married in heaven. Marriage is an earthly bond, and it is broken by physical death (see Romans 7:2 and 1 Timothy 5:14).

Most likely, there will be no marriage in heaven simply because there will be no need for it. For one thing, marriage on earth is a representation of Christ's relationship to the church (Ephesians 5:25–33; 2 Corinthians 11:2). In heaven, the representation will become reality (Revelation 19:6–8; 21:2). The image will no longer be needed as the shadow gives way to the substance (cf. Colossians 2:17).

Undoubtedly, marriage is not intended to be only an image; it has significant and practical purpose on earth. God established marriage in the Garden of Eden before the entrance of sin. So, marriage is part of God's good design for humanity on earth. After

He made the man, "The Lord God said, 'It is not good for the man to be alone. I will make a helper suitable for him'" (Genesis 2:18). The solution to the man being alone was the creation of the woman, and, specifically in this instance, the bond of marriage between Adam and Eve.

Marriage is the foundational building block of society. Within marriage God commanded procreation and the filling of the earth with human beings (Genesis 1:28). The man and woman together were needed to image God (Genesis 1:27) and fulfill His mandate (Genesis 1:28). In heaven, however, there will be no need for procreation. Heaven will be filled by those redeemed by the Lord Jesus Christ; the command to "be fruitful and multiply" will be lifted, and no babies will be born in heaven. The need for procreation will end in heaven, and the need for marriage will end at the same time.

But marriage is not solely about procreation. When God made the woman, "The man said, 'This is now bone of my bones and flesh of my flesh; she shall be called "woman," for she was taken out of man.' That is why a man leaves his father and mother and is united to his wife, and they become one flesh" (Genesis 2:23–24). Marriage is a unique partnership of two distinct, and yet like, humans. The woman was the perfect complement to the man to fulfill a God-given design (Genesis 2:18). Before sin entered the world, "Adam and his wife were both naked, and they felt no shame" (Genesis 2:25). Taking all this together, we see that marriage is designed for union, intimacy, and fruitfulness. In heaven, there will be no shame. And we will be in perfect union with God and with others (John 17:21–24; 1 Corinthians 13:12; Revelation 22:3–5). The intimacy many currently experience in marriage will be complete in a far greater way.

Marriage is a good gift, albeit a temporal one. It is the biblical norm and God's plan for the majority of people. On earth, marriage brings an opportunity for deep companionship and expression of self-sacrificial love, which are instructive about God's relationship with His people. It provides for practical needs like procreation.

In a fallen world, a loving marriage can be a place of refuge and strength. A marriage with God at the center can be a place of edification as well as a multiplier for effective kingdom work. But, in heaven, marriage will not be needed. In many ways, the single among us can serve to remind us of this heavenly reality. Marriage has a good earthly purpose, and it should be defended and cherished. But marriage is not intended for eternity; therefore, marriage will not continue into heaven.

Some worry that they will miss the intimacy, companionship, and pleasures of marriage in heaven. But that is to misunderstand the fullness of the Lord. We will be fully satisfied in heaven. Whatever we know as the best, most intense joys in this world, the joys of the next world will be greater still. In this world, we enjoy the sun, but the heavenly city "does not need the sun or the moon to shine on it, for the glory of God gives it light, and the Lamb is its lamp" (Revelation 21:23; cf. Isaiah 60:19). Just as the glory of God is infinitely greater than the physical sun, relationships in heaven will be infinitely more fulfilling than marriage in this world.

John Piper put it this way: "The pleasures of this world are foretastes and pointers to the inconceivably superior pleasures of the age to come. . . . Marriage ends because all its pleasures are preludes and pointers to something so much better that the human heart cannot imagine (1 Corinthians 2:9). . . . With every taste or every dream, remember: this is only foretaste—only prelude."[11]

59. Will there be sex in heaven?

The Bible does not address the topic of sex in heaven. Without a clear statement in Scripture on the matter, we can't really say yes or no about the possibility of sex in heaven. However, the Bible does address a related topic: marriage in heaven or, to be more precise, marriage after the resurrection.

In Matthew 22 the Sadducees attempt to discredit Jesus by asking what they considered a tough question about marriage and the resurrection. They came to Him and presented a hypothetical case in which a woman had been married multiple times in her life. Then they asked which husband would be hers in the resurrection: "Whose wife will she be . . . , since all of them were married to her?" (verse 28). Jesus answered them with these words: "At the resurrection people will neither marry nor be given in marriage; they will be like the angels in heaven" (verse 30).

The fact that there is no marriage in heaven suggests that there is no sex in heaven, although the Lord does not draw that explicit conclusion. The plain teaching of Jesus in Matthew 22:29–32 is 1) resurrection will take place and 2) marriage will no longer be part of our experience. It seems that marriage is a relationship to be enjoyed in this life, but it will not carry forward into the next life. We do not lose our identity in heaven (see Luke 16:23), but we will not hold the same relationships that we do on earth. Our existence will be quite different from what we are used to here and now.

From the fact that there is no marriage in heaven we surmise at least two other things:

1) There will be no procreation in heaven. The number of the redeemed is set, and, with no death, there will be no need to propagate the human race.

2) There will be no sexual intercourse in heaven. The appetites and desires of this world will give way to higher and infinitely more gratifying delights in the world to come.

There will be no need for sex in heaven, just as there will be no need for many other things. For centuries, the temple in Jerusalem and the sacrifices offered there were at the heart of worship, but, once Christ offered Himself as the ultimate sacrifice, the temple and the sacrificial system were no longer needed (John 4:22–23). They had been "copies of the heavenly things" (Hebrews 9:23). In the same way, the marriage relationship is a picture of our relationship with Christ (Ephesians 5:31–32). Once we are present with Christ, the illustration will no longer be needed. We will have the reality, which is far better than any earthly representation. This is why Jesus is called the Bridegroom, the church is called His bride, and our celebration in heaven is called the wedding (John 3:29; Matthew 22:1–14; Revelation 19:7–9).

SECTION 7
Questions about Hell

60. Does hell exist?

Yes, hell exists, according to the Bible. *Note: in the remainder of this article, we will use the term* hell *to mean, broadly, "place of conscious torment after death." We realize that hell is technically different from the lake of fire, but we will allow our other articles to describe the differences.*

The Bible speaks of the reality of hell in the same terms as the reality of heaven (Revelation 20:14–15; 21:1–2). The concept of a real, conscious, forever-and-ever existence in hell is just as biblical as a real, conscious, forever-and-ever existence in heaven. To deny one while accepting the other is simply illogical from a biblical standpoint.

Despite the Bible's clear teaching of both heaven and hell, it is not unusual for people to believe in the reality of heaven while rejecting the reality of hell. In part, this is due to wishful thinking.

It's easier to accept the idea of a "nice" afterlife, but damnation isn't quite so appealing. This is the same mistake human beings often make when it comes to substance abuse, dangerous behaviors, and so forth. The assumption that we will get what we want overrides the unpleasant (but rational) view that things might not end well.

Rejection of the existence of hell can also be blamed on inaccurate assumptions about what hell is. Hell is frequently imagined as a burning wasteland, a dungeon full of cauldrons and pitchforks, or an underground city filled with ghosts and goblins. Popular depictions of hell often involve a flaming torture chamber or a spiritual jail where evil things reside—and where good things travel to battle evil. This version of hell does not exist. There is a real place called hell, but it is not the Dantesque image most people think of. Certain details about hell are given in the Bible, but those details do not match the popular myths.

The Bible gives few particulars about hell. We know that it was originally intended for demonic spiritual beings, not people (Matthew 25:41). The experience of being in hell is compared to burning (Mark 9:43; 9:48; Matthew 18:9; Luke 16:24). At the same time, hell is compared to darkness (Matthew 22:13) and is associated with intense grief (Matthew 8:12) and horror (Mark 9:48).

In short, the Bible tells us only what being in hell is like; it does not explicitly say what hell is or how exactly it functions. What the Bible does make clear is that hell is real, eternal, and to be avoided at all costs (Matthew 5:29–30).

61. Did God create hell?

Hell is a place of suffering originally prepared by God for the devil and his angels (Matthew 18:9; 25:41). The words *Hades* (Greek) and *Sheol* (Hebrew) are sometimes associated with hell. However, Hades/Sheol is simply the place or realm where the spirits of people go when they die (see Genesis 37:35). Hades/Sheol is not necessarily a place of torment because God's people were said to go there as well as the wicked. In the New Testament, we find that Hades is somehow "compartmentalized." That is, the realm of the dead is divided into a place of comfort and a place of torment (Luke 16:19–31).

There are other words associated with hell in the Bible, such as *Gehenna* and *lake of fire*. The biblical teaching is that there is an actual place where the spirits of the unsaved go for eternity (Revelation 9:1; 20:15; Matthew 23:33).

Everything that ever was or is or will be is created by God, including hell (Colossians 1:16). John 1:3 says, "All things were made through him, and without him was not any thing made that was made" (ESV). God alone has the power to cast someone into hell (Luke 12:5). Jesus holds the keys of death and Hades (Revelation 1:18).

Jesus said that hell was "prepared" for Satan and the demons (Matthew 25:41). Hell is a just punishment for the wicked one. The lake of fire will be the destination for those who reject Christ (2 Peter 2:4–9). The good news is that people can avoid hell. God, in His infinite mercy and love, has offered salvation by grace through faith in God's Son, Jesus Christ (John 3:16, 36; 5:24).

62. What was Jesus' teaching on hell?

If there's one doctrine that people would rather ignore, suppress, or wish away, it's the teaching of hell. But there's no way around it—if you take the Bible at all seriously, you must believe in a literal hell. Our Lord Jesus Himself taught frequently about hell—in fact, we learn far more about hell from Jesus' words than from any other part of Scripture.

Jesus spoke of hell in Mark 9:43–48, using a valley called "*Gehenna*" as a metaphor. This valley, called "Topheth" or "the Valley of Ben Hinnom" in the Old Testament, had been desecrated by human sacrifice (2 Kings 23:10). Jeremiah linked the valley to God's judgment, prophesying that one day it would be called "the Valley of Slaughter" (Jeremiah 7:31–32). Isaiah associated the same valley with divine fire: "Its fire pit has been made deep and wide, with an abundance of fire and wood; the breath of the LORD, like a stream of burning sulfur, sets it ablaze" (Isaiah 30:33). Jesus mentioned fire in relation to hell at least twenty times (e.g., Matthew 5:22; 18:9). He also spoke of hell as "outer darkness" (Matthew 8:12 ESV).

Jesus consistently contrasted hell with the kingdom of God. Hell is the only alternative to an eternity spent in God's kingdom. It is the opposite of perfect fellowship with God forever. We will summarize Jesus' teaching related to hell with five words: *reality*, *rebellion*, *regret*, *relentlessness*, and *reconciliation*:

- *Reality*: Jesus taught that hell is a real place where some beings will spend eternity (Matthew 23:33; 25:41; Mark 9:43). In Jesus' teaching, hell is not figurative or symbolic; it is a real place in which real experiences take place. Jesus portrayed hell with vivid imagery such as fire and darkness (Matthew 5:22; 8:8–12).

- *Rebellion*: According to Jesus, hell is a place for those who reject God, who rebel against His kingship and refuse His grace. Jesus' parables consistently portray people rejecting God's invitation to fellowship, and the only alternative to fellowship with God is an eternity in hell (Matthew 22:1–14; Luke 14:15–24). All sin is some form of rebellion against God, and hell is the just punishment for sin (Matthew 5:22). The devil and his minions are the original rebels against God, and they will suffer eternally in hell, a place specially prepared for them (Matthew 25:41).

- *Regret*: Jesus does not portray hell as a pleasant place or even a neutral state. To the contrary, it is a place of torment (Mark 9:48). As the dark place outside of God's kingdom of light, hell is full of pain and regret. "There will be weeping and gnashing of teeth" (Matthew 13:42; see also Matthew 22:13; 24:51; Luke 13:28).

- *Relentlessness*: Based on Jesus' teaching, hell is not temporary, but eternal. Those who suffer in hell will suffer forever. "The fire never goes out," Jesus said (Mark 9:48 NLT; cf. Matthew 25:46). There is no exit from hell, and no respite from it or comfort in it (see Luke 16:19–31).

- *Reconciliation*: Thankfully, there is one way to escape hell *before entering*. God offers us reconciliation with Him, so that we never have to experience hell. That reconciliation was made possible through the death and resurrection of His Son, Jesus Christ. Jesus, the One who warned us about hell so often, is the One who saves us from hell. Through faith in Christ, anyone can be reconciled to God, apart from personal merit or virtue. Jesus gives the promise, "Very truly I tell you, whoever hears my word and believes him who sent me has eternal life and will not be judged but has crossed over from death to life" (John 5:24).

For God so loved the world that he gave his one and only Son, that whoever believes in him shall not perish but have eternal life. For God did not send his Son into the world to condemn the world, but to save the world through him. Whoever believes in him is not condemned, but whoever does not believe stands condemned already because they have not believed in the name of God's one and only Son.

John 3:16–18

If you have not trusted Him yet, don't delay any longer. Turn to Him today because someday it will be too late.

63. What is the difference between Sheol, Hades, Gehenna, hell, the lake of fire, paradise, and Abraham's bosom?

The different terms used in the Bible for heaven and hell—*Sheol, Hades, Gehenna,* the *lake of fire, paradise,* and *Abraham's bosom*—are the subject of some debate and can be hard to keep straight.

The word *paradise* is used as a synonym for *heaven* (2 Corinthians 12:3–4; Revelation 2:7). When Jesus was dying on the cross and one of the thieves being crucified with Him asked Him for mercy, Jesus replied, "Truly I tell you, today you will be with me in paradise" (Luke 23:43). Jesus knew that His death was imminent and that He would soon be in heaven with His Father. In His words of comfort to the penitent thief, Jesus used *paradise* as a synonym for *heaven,* and the word has come to be associated with any place of ideal loveliness and delight.

Abraham's bosom is referred to only once in the Bible—in the story of Lazarus and the rich man (Luke 16:19–31). *Abraham's lap* was used in the Talmud as a synonym for *heaven.*[12] The image in Jesus' story is of Lazarus reclining at a table leaning on Abraham's breast at the heavenly banquet—as John leaned on Jesus' breast at the Last Supper. The point of the story is that wicked men will see the righteous in a happy state, while they themselves are in torment, and that a "great gulf" that can never be spanned exists between them (Luke 16:26 NKJV). Abraham's bosom is obviously a place of peace, rest, and joy—in other words, paradise.

In the Hebrew Scriptures, the word used to denote the realm of the dead is *Sheol.* It simply means "the place of the dead" or "the place of departed souls/spirits." The New Testament Greek equivalent to *Sheol* is *Hades,* which is also a general reference to "the place of the dead." Sheol/Hades is divided into a place of blessing (where Lazarus was in Luke 16) and a place of torment (where the rich man was in Luke 16). Sheol also seems to be a temporary place where souls are kept as they await the final resurrection. The souls of the righteous, at death, go directly into the presence of God—the part of Sheol called "heaven," "paradise," or "Abraham's bosom" (Luke 23:43; 2 Corinthians 5:8; Philippians 1:23).

The Greek word *Gehenna* is used in the New Testament for "hell" (see Matthew 5:29; 23:33). The word is derived from the Hebrew word *Ge-hinnom*, which designated a valley south of Jerusalem—a cursed place that had been the site of human sacrifice (2 Chronicles 28:3; 33:6). Jesus referenced Gehenna as a symbol of the place of judgment after death, alluding to prophecies in Jeremiah 19:6 and Isaiah 30:33.

The lake of fire, mentioned only in Revelation 19:20 and 20:10, 14–15, is the final hell, the place of eternal punishment for all unrepentant rebels, both angelic and human (Matthew 25:41). It is described as a place of burning sulfur, and those in it experience eternal, unspeakable agony of an unrelenting nature (Luke 16:24; Mark 9:45–46). Those in Hades/Sheol who have rejected Christ will have the lake of fire as their final destination.

But those whose names are written in the Lamb's Book of Life should have no fear of this terrible fate. By faith in Christ and His blood shed on the cross for our sins, we are destined to live eternally in the blessed presence of God.

64. Why is the idea of eternal damnation so repulsive to many people?

In the shifting winds of modern culture, the idea of everlasting torment and damnation is difficult for many people to accept. Admittedly, the concept of an eternal hell is not a pleasant thought. Most people would rather not think about the possibility of a never-ending judgment from God.

Despite the aversion many people have to the idea of eternal damnation, the Bible teaches that hell is a literal place. And it's not only Satan and his minions who will be punished there; *everyone* who rejects Jesus Christ will spend eternity in the lake of fire (Revelation 20:15). Reinterpreting Scripture to explain away eternal damnation will not change the facts. Rejecting the doctrine of hell will not mitigate its flames. Still, many people are repulsed by the idea of an eternal hell. Here are some reasons for their rejection of this doctrine:

The influence of contemporary thought. In this postmodern era, many go to great lengths to assure no one is offended, and the doctrine of hell is no doubt offensive to the natural man. The doctrine of hell is often deemed too harsh, too old-fashioned, or too insensitive for publication. The wisdom of this world is focused on this life, with no thought of the afterlife.

Fear. Never-ending, conscious punishment devoid of any hope is indeed a frightening prospect. Many people would rather ignore the fear than face it and deal with it truthfully. The fact is, hell *should be* frightening, considering it is the place of judgment originally created for the devil and his angels (Matthew 25:41).

A flawed view of God's love. Many who reject the idea of eternal damnation do so because they find it difficult to believe that a loving God could banish people to a place as horrific as hell for all eternity. However, God's love does not negate His justice, His righteousness, nor His holiness. Neither does His justice negate His love. In fact, God's love has provided the way to escape His wrath: the sacrifice of Jesus Christ on the cross (John 3:16–18).

A downplaying of sin. Some find it unfair that the recompense for a mere *lifetime* of sinning should be an *eternal* punishment. Others reject the idea of hell because, in their minds, sin isn't all that bad. Certainly not bad enough to warrant eternal torture. Of course, it is usually our *own* sin that we downplay; *other* people might deserve hell—murderers and the like. This attitude reveals a misunderstanding of the universally heinous nature of sin. The problem is an insistence on our own basic goodness, which precludes thoughts of a fiery judgment and denies the truth of Romans

3:10 ("There is no one righteous, not even one"). The enormity of our iniquity compelled Christ to the cross. God hated sin to death.

Alternate theories. Another reason people reject the concept of eternal damnation is that they have been taught something different. One alternative theory is universalism, which says that everyone will eventually make it to heaven. Another is annihilationism, in which the existence of hell is acknowledged but its eternal nature is denied. Annihilationists believe that those who end up in hell will eventually die and cease to exist (i.e., they will be annihilated). According to this theory, hell is a temporary punishment.

Incomplete teaching. Many contemporary pastors who *do* believe in the doctrine of hell consider it simply too delicate a subject to preach on. This further contributes to the modern denial of hell. Congregants in churches where hell is not preached are often ignorant of what the Bible says on the subject and are prime candidates for deception on the issue. Part of a pastor's responsibility is "to contend for the faith that was once for all entrusted to God's holy people" (Jude 1:3), not pick and choose what parts of the Bible to leave out.

Satan's ploys. Satan's first lie was a denial of judgment. In the Garden of Eden, the serpent told Eve, "You will not surely die" (Genesis 3:4 ESV). Denying the reality of judgment is still one of Satan's main tactics. "The god of this age has blinded the minds of unbelievers" (2 Corinthians 4:4), and the blindness he produces includes a denial of God's holy decrees. Convince the unsaved that there is no judgment, and they can "eat, drink and be merry" (Luke 12:19) with no care for the future.

If we understand the nature of God, we should have no difficulty accepting the concept of hell. "[God] is the Rock, his works are *perfect*, and all his ways are *just*. A faithful God who *does no wrong, upright and just is he*" (Deuteronomy 32:4, emphasis added). Our just and perfect God created hell to eternally quarantine sin and bring an end to its devastation. Yes, God is love (1 John 4:8), and

His desire is that no one perish (2 Peter 3:9), but His love does not exist independent of His other attributes. We cannot sift divine holiness out of divine love without destroying both.

To contradict the Bible's teaching on hell is to say, essentially, "If *I* were God, I would not make hell like that." Such a thought is inherently prideful—it suggests that we can improve on God's plan. But we are not wiser than God; we are not more loving or more just.

Albert Mohler wrote, "There are particular doctrines that are especially odious and repulsive to the modern and postmodern mind. The traditional doctrine of hell as a place of everlasting punishment bears that scandal in a particular way. The doctrine is offensive to modern sensibilities and an embarrassment to many who consider themselves to be Christians. Those Friedrich Schlei-ermacher called the 'cultured despisers of religion' especially despise the doctrine of hell. As one observer has quipped, hell must be air-conditioned."[13] The sad irony is, attempts to "air condition" hell only serve to send more people there.

65. How is eternity in hell a fair punishment for sin?

Many people are uncomfortable, to say the least, with the idea of an eternal hell. This discomfort, though, is often the result of an incomplete understanding of three things: the nature of God, the nature of man, and the nature of sin. Hell will never be an easy topic, but its fairness can be understood.

As fallen, sinful human beings, we have difficulty grasping the nature of God. We tend to see God as a kind, merciful being whose love for us overrides and overshadows all His other attributes. Of course, God is loving, kind, and merciful, but He is also holy and righteous and just. His attributes exist *together* and cannot be separated from one another. In His holiness, He cannot tolerate sin (Proverbs 6:16–19). In His righteousness, He is angry with the wicked and disobedient (Isaiah 5:25; Hosea 8:5; Zechariah 10:3). In His justice, He must punish sin. If He failed to punish wrongdoing, God would be unjust.

All sin is ultimately against God (Psalm 51:4). It is a transgression of His law (1 John 3:4). God is infinite in His nature, infinite in glory, and infinite in worthiness. This makes Him infinitely worthy of obedience, and crimes committed against Him warrant an infinite penalty—eternity in hell.

Even under our human laws, the severity of a crime depends, in part, on the value of the target of the offense. If a man enters a junkyard at night and smashes the headlights of a derelict car, he will probably pay a small fine. But if that same man enters the showroom of a Porche dealer and whales away at the 911s, he will pay a much larger fine and probably serve some jail time. The difference is the value of the crime's target. Punishment is proportionate to the worth of the thing damaged. God's glory is the most valuable thing in existence—it is of infinite worth. If punishment is proportional, then crimes committed against God deserve an infinite penalty—eternity in hell.

In Jesus' story of the rich man and Lazarus, the rich man goes to hell after he dies while Lazarus goes to paradise (Luke 16). The rich man in hell is "in torment" (verse 23), but he never asks, "How did I end up here?" Neither does he say, "I don't deserve this" or "This is unfair." He only asks that someone go to his brothers who are still alive and warn them against his fate. The man in hell seemed to accept that his punishment was deserved and that his brothers deserved similar fates.

Like the rich man in Jesus' story, every sinner in hell has a full realization that he deserves to be there. Each sinner has a fully informed, acutely aware conscience that, in hell, becomes a torment. The undeniable guilt will produce everlasting shame, misery, regret, and self-hatred. There will be no relief from the despair.

The reality of eternal damnation is frightening. We are right to fear such a fate and be troubled by thoughts of it. But there is good news. God loves us to the extent that He sent His Son, Jesus, to provide the payment for our sin (John 3:16). When Jesus died on the cross, He took our punishment and satisfied God's righteous demand for justice. Because of His intrinsic, infinite worth, Jesus was able to cover the infinite debt we owed. All that remains is for us to confess our sin and place our faith in Christ's death and resurrection. Forgiveness of sin and salvation from eternal hell can be ours by grace, through faith.

66. How is an eternity in hell a just punishment for only a human lifetime of sin?

The Bible says that hell is eternal (Matthew 25:46). Many people struggle with the justice of that. They question how it is just for God to punish a person eternally for sinning only 70, 80, 90, or 100 years—however long they lived. How does a sinner's finite lifespan merit an infinitely long punishment?

There are two principles that lead us to believe eternity in hell is the just punishment for sin, no matter how long one's earthly life lasted.

First, the Bible declares that all sin is ultimately against God (Psalm 51:4). The extent of the punishment depends, in part, on the target of the crime. In a human court of law, a physical assault against an individual will usually result in a fine and possibly some time in jail. But a physical assault against the president or prime minister of a country will likely result in a lifetime in prison. And this is the case despite the fact that the crime was a one-time offense, not a continual, ongoing action. God is infinitely greater than any human being, and an assault on Him is infinitely worse than any crime committed against a human being. An attack on an infinitely worthy being merits an infinite punishment.

Second, it would seem that the unredeemed will continue to sin after death. Are those who go to hell suddenly sinless and perfect? No. Those who go into eternity without Christ will be confirmed in their wickedness. The hard-hearted will be eternally hard-hearted. There will be "weeping and gnashing of teeth" in hell (Matthew 25:30) but no repentance. Sinners in hell will be given over to their own nature; they will be sin-infected, evil, immoral, and depraved beings for all of eternity, forever unredeemed and unregenerate. The lake of fire will be a place of eternal rebellion against God—even as that rebellion is judged (Revelation 20:14–15; cf. Revelation 16:9, 11). Unsaved people do not "only" sin for 70, 80, 90, or 100 years. They sin for eternity.

Essentially, if a person wants to be separated from God for eternity, God will grant that desire. The will of the unsaved is to reject salvation through Jesus Christ and remain in sin; God will honor that decision and its consequences for eternity.

67. How can a loving God send someone to hell?

To address the question of how a loving God can send someone to hell, we need to define a few terms and, most likely, correct a few assumptions. We must first define the term *loving*. Our culture tends to think of *love* as a completely non-confrontational, tolerant approval of whatever the loved one wants to do. But that is not a biblical definition. Love, according to the Bible, is goodwill and benevolence shown in self-sacrifice and an unconditional commitment to the loved one. Love is action promoting the well-being of another person.

Implied in the question "how can a loving God send someone to hell?" is the assumption that sending someone to hell is unloving on God's part. But God's very nature is love (1 John 4:16). He cannot do anything that is unloving because His every action and every thought is an expression of His nature. God alone loves in the highest sense of the word; He loves with perfect freedom and objectivity.

If we say that God is somehow wrong to punish unrepentant sinners in the manner He has chosen, then we have declared that we are more loving than God is—and wiser and fairer and more righteous. But it is impossible for us to be more loving than Love Himself. And our feeble notions of what is "wise" and "fair" will always fall short of God's perfection.

Another assumption we must guard against in asking the question "how can a loving God send someone to hell?" concerns the word *send*. Yes, God is the one—the only one—who sends people to hell (Luke 12:5; Revelation 20:15). However, when someone is sent to hell, it is not a unilateral action on God's part, and the person being sent is not a passive victim of circumstance. God has given human beings freedom to participate in their life choices and eternal destinations (John 3:16–18). God has entrusted personal responsibility to each of us. And, in His love, God sent His only begotten Son into the world to save sinners. "God demonstrates his own love for us in this: While we were still sinners, Christ died for us" (Romans 5:8).

"How can a loving God send someone to hell?" Romans 1:18–20 lays the foundation for the answer: "The wrath of God is being revealed from heaven against all the godlessness and wickedness of people, who suppress the truth by their wickedness, since what may be known about God is plain to them, because God has made it plain to them. For since the creation of the world God's invisible qualities—his eternal power and divine nature—have been clearly seen, being understood from what has been made, so that *people are without excuse*" (emphasis added).

There are several key points in this passage. First, people actively "suppress the truth." Everyone has been given enough truth to know about God and surrender to Him, but they willfully refuse to accept the truth. They love darkness rather than light (John

3:19). Dr. Thomas Nagel, an atheistic professor of philosophy and law, has said, "It isn't just that I don't believe in God and, naturally, hope that I'm right in my belief. It's that I hope there is no God! I don't want there to be a God; I don't want the universe to be like that."[14]

Second, Romans 1:19 states that God has "made [the truth about God] plain to them." In other words, the Creator took the initiative to make His truth obvious to everyone. History has proved this since time began, as every culture and civilization has sought an understanding of a Creator to whom they owe allegiance. The innate understanding that God exists is due to our being created in the image of God (Genesis 1:27).

Third, Romans 1:20 says that people "have no excuse for not knowing God" (NLT). There is no defense, no justification for continuing to reject God's offer of salvation in Christ. In love, God gave each of us enough truth to turn toward Him rather than away from Him.

When considering the question "how can a loving God send someone to hell?" we must not try to separate God's love from His justice and righteousness. God's attributes exist *together*, and they cannot be plucked out and made to stand alone. God is love, and that shapes His justice; at the same time, His justice affects His expressions of love. Justice requires adequate payment for crimes committed; love requires the extension of grace to the criminal. The cross shows both justice and love. As Jesus died on the cross, He bore the punishment for sin that justice demanded, and He extended the grace of forgiveness to sinners. Thus, both the justice and love of God were at work. "Mercy and truth have met together; Righteousness and peace have kissed" (Psalm 85:10 NKJV).

The question "How can a loving God send someone to hell?" has a logical counterpart: "How can a just God send someone to heaven?" The answer to both questions is, again, the cross. For those who believe in Christ and accept His loving sacrifice on their behalf, God's justice falls on Jesus. For those who turn away from Christ and reject His sacrifice, God's justice falls on them.

Hell was originally created for the devil and his angels (Matthew 25:41). When humans joined the devil's rebellion against God, hell became their fate, too. But God, in His love, provided a way of escape. He proved His love at the cross of Christ. Those who are in Christ have been forgiven of their sin by the grace of God. But those who reject Christ are spurning God's love and refusing His offer of salvation. If we decline the payment offered by another, we must pay the price ourselves, and "the wages of sin is death" (Romans 6:23). Sinners are sent to hell, in spite of God's love, because they reject God's loving provision of a Savior.

Jesus revealed the heart of the Father when He lamented those who spurned salvation: "Jerusalem, Jerusalem, you who kill the prophets and stone those sent to you, how often I have longed to gather your children together, as a hen gathers her chicks under her wings, and you were not willing" (Matthew 23:37; see also Isaiah 5:1–7 and Hosea 7:13). Hell does not negate God's love any more than heaven negates God's justice. "So we are Christ's ambassadors; God is making his appeal through us. We speak for Christ when we plead, 'Come back to God!'" (2 Corinthians 5:20 NLT).

68. Why does God send people to hell?

The Bible says that God created hell for Satan and the wicked angels who rebelled in heaven, but there are people in hell also (Matthew 25:41). Both angelic beings and human beings are in hell for the same reason: sin (Romans 6:23).

Because God is completely righteous and morally perfect (Psalm 18:30), He always does what is right—there is no "darkness" in God, not the smallest speck of imperfection (1 John 1:5). God Himself is the standard for what is right, good, and moral. If it were not for God being the standard of moral perfection, created beings would have nothing to measure themselves against. The Bible teaches that anything falling short of God's perfection is sinful, and every human being who has ever lived since Adam's fall has committed sin (Romans 3:23). Because Adam sinned, the entire human race now has a sinful nature (Romans 5:12). But people do not go to hell because of Adam's sin; they go to hell because of their own sin, which they freely choose (James 1:13–16).

God is infinitely glorious and worthy of obedience, and all sins are fundamentally against God. For this reason, the only just punishment for sin—a violation of infinite glory—must also be infinite (see Matthew 25:46).

All who commit sin deserve to go to hell because they have failed to meet God's righteous standard; they have broken His law of moral perfection. If God did not send people to hell for breaking His laws, He would not be just (Psalm 7:11). An analogy is what happens in a court of law between a judge and a lawbreaker. A just judge will sentence the guilty according to the law. A judge who ignores the law, overlooks the crime, and releases the guilty would not be a just judge (Deuteronomy 32:4). Corrupt or incompetent judges contribute to a disordered society: "Justice is driven back, and righteousness stands at a distance; truth has stumbled in the streets, honesty cannot enter" (Isaiah 59:14). If God failed to execute justice, we would have an anarchic universe.

As the Son of Man, Jesus has the authority to judge the world (John 5:27). Jesus Himself is the standard of holiness and the only one worthy of executing judgment. He spoke of the necessity of heeding His message: "All who reject me and my message will be judged on the day of judgment by the truth I have spoken" (John 12:48 NLT).

The good news is that God has mercy on the sinner. He made a way for us to avoid the punishment of hell. Salvation is God's gift to those who trust in the atoning work of His Son, Jesus Christ (Romans 5:9). Believers are forgiven, and the penalty of their sin has been placed upon Christ on the cross (1 Peter 2:24). The sacrifice of Christ maintains God's justice—the sin is punished—and at the same time extends His mercy and grace to all who believe.

69. Does God love the people who are in hell?

This is an important question, and the short answer is "yes." God does love people in hell. But explaining this answer is fraught with difficulty on at least three points. First, hell is caricatured as silly or trifling in modern Western culture. Just think of how often hell is portrayed as an underground network of caves in which a bright red, horned devil lurks with a pitchfork.

Second, the concept of love has been contorted into an omnibus feeling-based idea to fit any fleeting object of human desire.

Third, many people conceive of God as a bearded old man sitting somewhere in the clouds, like a human with extra powers. We must disabuse ourselves of these points before we can understand how God can love people in hell.

Let us begin with the last point. If God is conceived of as a finite, creaturely personage, then the doctrine of divine justice will make little sense. His omniscience, perfection, justice, holiness, and goodness are not possible if God is not infinite and transcendent; finite beings cannot be essentially perfect, etc. But making God in the image of man is, unfortunately, what many people do. When we think God is just like us, but with superpowers, we commit a great error. God is not *a* being in the cosmos; He is *being* itself (Exodus 3:14; Acts 17:24–29). He transcends the cosmos. This is critical to the question of God loving people in hell, because, when 1 John 4:8 says, "God is love," it means the very essence of God is love. It does not mean that God loves His creation because it does something for Him or that He goes through mood changes, having good days and bad days. It does not mean that God is impacted by what happens in time. Rather, God loves people simply because that is who He *is*. Because of this, God's love is not affected by our actions or our location. God loves the people in hell.

The term *love*, in the Christian sense, concerns the willing of what is good for another. To will the good of someone is to first discern what would be good for him and then act toward that end. Love is not a passion or emotion, per se. When we say that God is love, we mean that the very nature of God is self-sacrificial love for others. This love was exemplified on the cross, where Jesus gave His life to give us eternal life (John 3:16). The divine essence knows and wills the good of all creatures.

Pop culture takes a cavalier approach to hell. People will casually tell people to go to hell or assume that hell will be a big party. In the biblical view, what is broadly called "hell" represents something quite abhorrent. The Bible says that, upon death, the wicked soul subsists in conscious torment until the future resurrection (see Luke 16:19–31). After the resurrection and final judgment, the wicked are cast into the lake of fire (Revelation 20:11–15). Whereas the righteous dwell with God eternally, the unrighteous are separated from God. This does not mean God's presence is unknown or absent; rather, the experience of God is different.

So how is it that God loves people in hell? In what way is He willing the good of those who are separated from Him?

It is good for the creature and Creator to be united, such as they were in the beginning (Genesis 1–2). Sin causes a fracture in that union. Sin can thus be seen as the inward turning away of creatures from their own good. Habitual sin becomes a reinforcing cycle of bending away from God. Without the healing and redemptive love of Christ bending the creatures back toward God, they will persist in their ruinous state. The creature can come to hate God in that he chooses to love himself and seek everything *but* God despite the reconciling goodness and grace extended to him in countless ways.

God loves His creation—His nature is love—but this love manifests itself differently to the impenitent creature and to the penitent. It is the same love, experienced from two perspectives. As an analogy, two people outside on a bright, sunny day can have very different experiences if one is in the sunshine and the other is in the shadow. In both cases, the sun is the same; it is the experience of the creatures that is different, depending on their situation relative to the sun. In a similar way, the creaturely experience of God is different in hell than it is in heaven. Instead of experiencing the fullness of God's grace, the one in hell gets the fullness of divine wrath.

70. What does it mean that hell is eternal separation from God?

The Bible is clear that there are two possible destinations for every human soul following physical death: heaven or hell (Matthew 25:34, 41, 46; Luke 16:22–23). Only the righteous inherit eternal life, and the only way to be declared righteous before God is through faith in the death and resurrection of Jesus Christ (John 3:16–18; Romans 10:9). The souls of the righteous go directly into the presence of God (Luke 23:43; 2 Corinthians 5:8; Philippians 1:23).

For those who do not receive Jesus Christ as Savior, death will result in everlasting punishment (2 Thessalonians 1:8–9). This punishment is described in a variety of ways: agony (Luke 16:24), a lake of fire (Revelation 20:14–15), outer darkness (Matthew 8:12 NKJV), and a prison (1 Peter 3:19), for example. This place of punishment is eternal (Jude 1:13; Matthew 25:46).

Second Thessalonians 1:8–9 associates hell with a separation from God: "He will punish those who do not know God and do not obey the gospel of our Lord Jesus. They will be punished with everlasting destruction and shut out from the presence of the Lord and from the glory of his might." The misery of hell will include not only physical torture, but also the agony of being separated from God in a way never experienced before. At the judgment,

Jesus will tell the wicked, "Depart from me" (Luke 13:27 ESV; cf. Psalm 6:8). Hell is where those sent away will go.

God is the source of all good things (James 1:17). To be separated from God is to be shut out from all exposure to anything good. It is to be excluded from every avenue of happiness. In this life, no one is totally separated from God. Everyone experiences divine blessing in some form: "[God] has not left himself without testimony: He has shown kindness by giving you rain from heaven and crops in their seasons; he provides you with plenty of food and fills your hearts with joy" (Acts 14:17; cf. Matthew 5:45). In hell, none of those blessings will be available. Hell will be devoid of all happiness, all comfort, all virtue, and all honor. If it's good, it will not be in hell.

Hell is characterized as the complete absence of goodness; righteousness will be lacking. After the judgment, the state of the wicked will be fixed and unchanging, with not a shred of goodness: "Let the one who does wrong continue to do wrong; let the vile person continue to be vile" (Revelation 22:11). Denizens of hell will thus be in a state of perpetual sinfulness, accompanied by a full understanding of sin's horrors. The remorse, guilt, and shame will be unending. And there will be no recourse, no rescue, because those in hell are eternally separated from the Savior.

To be separated from God in hell is to be forever cut off from light (1 John 1:5), love (1 John 4:8), joy (Matthew 25:23), and peace (Ephesians 2:14) because God is the source of all those good things. Any good we observe in humanity today is merely a reflection of the character of God, in whose image we were created (Genesis 1:27).

The spirits of those regenerated by God's Holy Spirit will abide forever with God in a perfected state (1 John 3:2), but the opposite is true of those in hell. Those who die in their sins will exist forever apart from God in a sinful state. Their separation from God will be irreversible. Those in hell have forever lost the chance to see God's face, hear His voice, experience His forgiveness, or enjoy His fellowship. To be forever separated from God is the ultimate punishment.

SECTION 8
Questions about What Hell Will Be Like

71. What does the Bible say about hell?

There is sometimes confusion about use of the term *hell* as the temporary gathering place of the dead (also known as Sheol or Hades). This article will focus on one common usage of the word *hell* as being synonymous with the lake of fire, the eternal place of punishment reserved for the lost.

If heaven is vastly misunderstood thanks to misconceptions and falsehoods perpetuated by myth and popular culture, the realities of hell are all the more misunderstood. Medieval art, fanciful literature, and biblical illiteracy may be the top three reasons why the average person's understanding of hell is clouded with ignorance and fallacies. Compounding the problem, many pastors and Bible teachers avoid discussing hell for fear of upsetting their congregants. Indeed, hell is a most unpleasant topic, but since our Lord Jesus taught on hell, we should not remain silent on the matter. According to the Bible, hell is real (Mark 9:43), it is where sinners are punished (Matthew 5:22), it is a place of torment (Revelation 14:11), and it is eternal (Mark 9:48). Hell was originally created for Satan and his angels (Matthew 25:41).

Dispelling some of the more prevalent myths about hell is useful in adding to our biblical understanding:

Myth 1: The devil's headquarters are in hell. The devil is not in hell now. Hell, or the lake of fire (also referred to as the second death), will receive its first occupants at the end of our Lord Jesus' millennial reign (Revelation 20:7–10). Also, hell is a place of torment (Luke 16:23–24; Revelation 20:10), so cartoonish images of prancing devils brandishing pitchforks while merrily dancing around a ring of fire are nonsensical. Rather than partying with his legions of demons, Satan will languish in hell.

Myth 2: Hell is reserved solely for the worst of evildoers such as cruel dictators and serial killers. While there are likely degrees of eternal punishment (Luke 12:47–49), all who refuse God's mercy must endure His wrath (John 3:18). There is heaven, and there is hell; there is no third option. While this reality makes the average person uncomfortable, there will be more unrepentant barbers, plumbers, middle school teachers, bricklayers, airline pilots, and accountants in hell than tyrants such as Hitler, Stalin, and Mao. Stalin will not be sent to the lake of fire because he murdered millions of his own countrymen; rather, Stalin, like the unrepentant librarian, will suffer in hell because he scorned God's mercy and rejected Christ.

Myth 3: A loving God would not send people to hell. If, by "love," one means an indulgent, enabling, misguided sort of sentimental affection, then there would be no eternal punishment. But God is not to be confused with a drowsy old man who winks at his grandchildren's mischievous antics from a rocking chair. God is just (Romans 12:19), and He will repay evil with affliction

(2 Thessalonians 1:6). Rather than accusing God of being cruel, we should remember hell is reserved for those who, by their own volition, snubbed God's mercy (Hebrews 2:3). Salvation is a gift free for the asking (Ephesians 2:8–9), but the world is filled with those whose minds and hearts are so full of earthly matters they haven't any room for what God would gladly give them. Ultimately, hell will prove to be a place for those who were willing to settle for less than God's best.

Myth 4: A just God would not send people to hell. Of all the arguments against hell, this may be the weakest. Where else would a just God send rebels who stubbornly and steadfastly refused to repent of their evil? Even in our own sometimes corrupt criminal justice system, lawbreakers are sent to prison. Should a just God reward hardened evildoers with eternal bliss? The Judge of all the earth will do what is right (Genesis 18:25). Additionally, those who will occupy hell will be those who avoided contact, companionship, and communication with the One who made them. Why should we think the unrepentant sinner who ran from the presence of God here on earth would be happy in His intimate company in heaven? Hell will be populated by people who chose to be there. To reject the Lord of heaven is to choose hell.

Myth 5: Hell is merely a scare tactic to enforce a particular brand of allegiance or behavior. If hell is real, then we will do well to fear it, and if hell is only a scare tactic, then might the same be said of warnings against tobacco use, drinking and driving, or income tax fraud? Jesus warned of the dangers of hell (Matthew 10:28). Would He have alerted us to the dangers of hell if the dangers were not real? Are those who deny hell's existence wiser, smarter, and better informed than the Son of God? To deny the perils of hell is to cast doubt on the words of our Savior.

Hell is a place of misery and suffering; hell is where torment and anguish never cease (Revelation 14:11). Whether the flames are literal or symbolic of some even greater woe, we can be certain that all this world has to offer—money, fame, reputation, power, or sexual gratification—is hardly worth the forfeiture of our eternal souls (Mark 8:36–38).

God takes no pleasure in the death of the wicked (Ezekiel 18:32). He finds no satisfaction in those who choose hell over Him. On the contrary, God loved the world so much that He sent His Son to rescue and redeem us (John 3:16). Jesus' death and resurrection are good news for lost sinners willing to believe that our sin debt has been paid in full. Those who receive God's grace through faith will live forever with Him.

Jesus is the best God can give us. God has nothing greater to offer than His Son. Those who have placed their faith in Jesus Christ have no reason to fear death and the grave; on the contrary, the best is yet to come. Yet there are those whose hearts are hardened and are more interested in gaining what the world has to offer. What a tragedy this is, for Christ has overcome sin, death, and hell on our behalf.

72. What does hell look like? How hot is hell?

We cannot know exactly what hell looks like or how hot it will be. But Scripture does use some descriptive language of hell, and that gives us an idea of what hell will be like. It is sure to be a place of torment, which the Bible often pictures as fiery. For the purposes of this article, the terms *hell* and *lake of fire* are used interchangeably.

Some interpreters take the Bible's descriptions of hell to be symbolic, because some of the descriptions are difficult to reconcile with each other. For example, picturing hell as both fire (Matthew 25:41) and outer darkness (Matthew 8:12) seems paradoxical. Of course, the God of the impossible can do anything, including make dark fire. So, the descriptions could be literal. Even if the language describing hell is symbolic, the place itself is real—and the reality will no doubt be worse than the symbols.

The scriptural descriptions of hell are meant to emphasize the torment and suffering that will be experienced by those sent there. The "fire" may picture the wrath of God that is experienced by unbelievers in hell, whereas the "outer darkness" may picture the alienation from God's love, mercy, and grace. Whether the vivid language is symbolic or literal, we can be assured that hell is a terrible, terrifying place. Possibly the most terrifying aspect of hell is its duration. The suffering is eternal. It has no end. For us, here and now, the concept of hell should drive us to the cross of Christ. It is only by repentance and faith in Christ that we can be saved from the wrath to come.

Here are some of the passages that describe hell:

Matthew 25:41: "Then he will say to those on his left, 'Depart from me, you who are cursed, into the eternal fire prepared for the devil and his angels.'"

Matthew 8:12 NKJV: "But the sons of the kingdom will be cast out into outer darkness. There will be weeping and gnashing of teeth."

Second Thessalonians 1:6–9: "God is just: He will pay back trouble to those who trouble you and give relief to you who are troubled, and to us as well. This will happen when the Lord Jesus is revealed from heaven in blazing fire with his powerful angels. He will punish those who do not know God and do not obey the gospel of our Lord Jesus. They will be punished with everlasting destruction and shut out from the presence of the Lord and from the glory of his might."

Revelation 20:10, 15: "And the devil, who deceived them, was thrown into the lake of burning sulfur, where the beast and the false prophet had been thrown. They will be tormented day and night for ever and ever. . . . Anyone whose name was not found written in the book of life was thrown into the lake of fire."

Romans 2:8: "But for those who are self-seeking and who reject the truth and follow evil, there will be wrath and anger."

Matthew 25:30: "And throw that worthless servant outside, into
the darkness, where there will be weeping and gnashing of teeth."

Hell, although we do not know exactly what it will look like, will
be a place of unending suffering and torment from which there
will be no escape. Therefore, now is the day of salvation. Now is
the day for all to repent and believe the gospel. Now is the day for
us to proclaim the good news that Christ has come to save sinners
who trust in Him for forgiveness. Those who look to Christ now
will be saved from the wrath to come (1 Thessalonians 1:9–10).

73. What does it mean that hell is referred to as a lake of fire?

The lake of fire is a term used in only a few verses near the end of
the Bible in the book of Revelation (19:20; 20:10, 14, 15; 21:8).
Jesus refers to Gehenna/hell several times (Matthew 10:28; Mark
9:43; Luke 12:5), as well as an "outer darkness" (Matthew 8:12
NKJV; 22:13 NKJV). These all seem to be different references to
the same thing. *Hell, the lake of fire,* and *outer darkness* are all
terms describing the final destination of those who reject Christ.
This is a state of complete separation from God, never-ending
and inescapable.

According to the Bible, the lake of fire is the "second death"
(Revelation 20:14). This is the ultimate consequence of sin, which
is to be totally cut off from God. The lake of fire will be a place of
perpetual suffering and misery. Scripture indicates that every person whose name is not in the book of life will be cast into the lake
of fire (Revelation 20:15). The lake of fire will also be the fate of the
beast and false prophet from the end times (Revelation 19:20), as
well as Satan himself (Revelation 20:10). The Bible indicates that
both death and Hades—the temporary destination of the unsaved
dead—will also be cast into the lake of fire (Revelation 20:14).

Even though hell is described using terminology such as fire and flame, it is not meant to be thought of as "only" a physical place. Hell is described as a place of "torment," not "torture," initially intended for purely spiritual beings (Matthew 25:41). In fact, the worst aspect of hell is an eternity of conscious, guilty, shameful separation from God and all forms of goodness. In that sense, hell is far worse than a literal inferno; a purely physical hell would not be as terrible as what the Bible describes.

In other words, the Bible tells us what hell is "like," using symbols such as the lake of fire. But Scripture does not tell us too much about what hell "is," in direct terms.

Fire is often used as a symbol of God's judgment. The symbolism stems from real-life examples of God's use of fire to punish the wicked—the overthrow of Sodom and Gomorrah (Genesis 19:24), for example, and the destruction of Elijah's enemies (2 Kings 1:12). Prophets associated God or His throne with a stream of fire, a symbol of His holy punishment of sin (e.g., Daniel 7:10; Isaiah 30:33). The fact that the destiny of those who reject God is pictured as a "lake of fire" speaks to how serious the judgment is. When God finally abolishes sin and death, all sinners will be condemned to the worst possible fate, described in the Bible using the most horrific terms.

74. Is hell literally a place of fire and brimstone?

By raining down fire and brimstone upon the cities of Sodom and Gomorrah, God not only demonstrated how He felt about overt sin, but He also launched an enduring metaphor. After the events of Genesis 19:24 (KJV), the mere mention of fire, brimstone, or Sodom and Gomorrah conjures up images of God's judgment. A "fire and brimstone preacher," also called a "hellfire preacher," is one who emphasizes God's fiery judgment, often with lurid descriptions and over-the-top presentations.

Fire and brimstone is an emotionally potent symbol, however, and has trouble escaping its own gravity. This fiery metaphor can impede, rather than advance, its purpose. A symbol should show a similarity between two *dissimilar* entities. Fire and brimstone describes some of what hell is *like*—but not all of what hell *is*.

The word the Bible uses to describe a burning hell—*Gehenna*—comes from an actual place, the valley of Gehenna adjacent to Jerusalem on the south. *Gehenna* is an English transliteration of the Greek form of an Aramaic word, which is derived from the Hebrew phrase "the Valley of (the son[s] of) Hinnom." In one of their greatest apostasies, the Jews (especially under kings Ahaz and Manasseh) burned their children in sacrifice to the god Molech in that very valley (2 Kings 16:3; 2 Chronicles 33:6; Jeremiah 32:35). Later, King Josiah desecrated the pagan altar there to prevent it from ever being used again for abominable sacrifices (2 Kings 23:10). So, in Jesus' day Gehenna had a history of uncleanness, demonic activity, and grotesque rituals—a fitting metaphor for hell.

In Mark 9:43 Jesus used another powerful image to illustrate the seriousness of hell: "If your hand causes you to sin, cut it off; it is better for you to enter life maimed, than, having your two hands, to go into hell, into the unquenchable fire" (NASB). For most readers, this image *does* escape its own gravity—in spite of the goriness! Few believe that Jesus wants us to literally cut off our own hands. He would *rather* that we do whatever is necessary to avoid going to hell, and that is the purpose of such language—to polarize, to set up an either/or dynamic, to compare. Since the first part of the verse (about amputation) uses hyperbolic imagery, it could be that the second part (about fire) does also. In any case, we should probably not take Mark 9:43 as an encyclopedic description of hell.

In addition to a place of fire, the New Testament describes hell as a bottomless pit or abyss (Revelation 20:3), a lake (Revelation 20:14), darkness (Matthew 25:30), death (Revelation 2:11), destruction (2 Thessalonians 1:9), everlasting torment (Revelation 20:10), a place of wailing and gnashing of teeth (Matthew 25:30), and a place of gradated punishment (Matthew 11:20–24; Luke 12:47–48; Revelation 20:12–13). The very *variety* of hell's descriptors argues against applying a literal interpretation to any particular one. The variety and symbolic nature of descriptors do not lessen hell, however—just the opposite. Their combined effect is to present a hell that is *worse* than death, *darker* than darkness, and *deeper* than any abyss. Hell is a place with *more* wailing and gnashing of teeth than any single descriptor could portray. Its symbolic descriptors bring us to a place beyond the limits of our language—to a place far worse than we could ever imagine.

75. Where is hell?

Various theories on the location of hell have been put forward. A traditional view is that hell is in the center of the earth. Others propose that hell is located in outer space in a black hole. In the Old Testament, the word translated "hell" is *Sheol*; in the New Testament, it's *Hades* (meaning "unseen") and *Gehenna* ("the Valley of Hinnom"). *Sheol* is also translated as "pit" and "grave." Both *Sheol* and *Hades* refer to a temporary abode of the dead before judgment (Psalm 9:17; Revelation 1:18). *Gehenna* refers to an eternal state of punishment for the wicked dead (Mark 9:43).

The idea that hell is below us, perhaps in the center of the earth, comes from passages such as Luke 10:15: "And thou, Capernaum, which art exalted to heaven, shalt be thrust down to hell" (KJV). Also, in 1 Samuel 28:13–15, the medium of Endor sees the spirit of Samuel "coming up out of the earth." We should note, however, that neither of these passages is concerned with the geographic location of hell. Capernaum's being thrust "down" is probably a reference to their being condemned rather than a physical direction. And the medium's vision of Samuel was just that: a vision.

In the King James Version, Ephesians 4:9 says that, before Jesus ascended into heaven, "he also descended . . . into the lower parts of the earth." Some Christians take "the lower parts of the earth" as a reference to hell, where they say Jesus spent the time between His death and resurrection. However, the New International Version gives a better translation: "He also descended to the lower, earthly regions." This verse simply says that Jesus came to earth. It's a reference to His incarnation, not to His location after death.

The notion that hell is somewhere in outer space, possibly in a black hole, is based on the knowledge that black holes are places of great heat and pressure from which nothing, not even light, can escape. Surprisingly, this concept of hell is presented in the 1979 Walt Disney film *The Black Hole*. Near the movie's end, all the characters pass through a black hole. On the other side, the villain finds himself in a fiery place of torment, while the other characters enjoy disembodied bliss. It's interesting that a Disney movie would include a depiction of hell, but it's best not to base our theology on movies!

Another speculation is that the earth itself will be the "lake of fire" spoken of in Revelation 20:10–15. When the earth is destroyed by fire (2 Peter 3:10; Revelation 21:1), the theory goes, God will use that burning sphere as the everlasting place of torment for the ungodly. Again, this is speculation.

To sum up, Scripture does not tell us the geological (or cosmological) location of hell. Hell is a literal place of real torment, but we do not know where it is. Hell may have a physical location in this universe, or it may be in an entirely different dimension. Whatever the case, the location of hell is far less important than the need to avoid going there.

76. Are there different levels of punishment in hell?

The idea that there are different levels of punishment in hell is graphically portrayed in *The Divine Comedy*, written by Dante

Alighieri between 1308 and 1321. In that poem, the Roman poet Virgil guides Dante through the nine circles of hell. The circles are concentric, representing a gradual increase in wickedness, and culminating at the center of the earth, where Satan is held in bondage. Each circle's sinners are punished in a fashion befitting their crimes. Each sinner is afflicted for all of eternity by the chief sin he committed. According to Dante, the circles range from the first circle, where the unbaptized and virtuous pagans dwell, to the very center of hell reserved for those who have committed the ultimate sin—treachery against God.

Although the Bible does not *specifically* say there are different levels of punishment in hell, it does seem to indicate that the judgment will indeed be experienced differently for different people. In Revelation 20:11–15, the people are judged "according to what they had done as recorded in the books" (Revelation 20:12). All the people at this judgment, though, are thrown into the lake of fire (Revelation 20:13–15). So, perhaps, the purpose of the judgment is to determine how severe the punishment in hell will be.

A clearer passage is Luke 10, where Jesus speaks of comparative punishment. First, Jesus says this about a village that rejects the gospel: "I tell you, it will be more bearable on that day for Sodom than for that town" (verse 12). Then He speaks to Bethsaida and Chorazin: "It will be more bearable for Tyre and Sidon at the judgment than for you" (verse 14). Whatever punishment the former residents of Sodom, Tyre, and Sidon were experiencing in hell, the Galilean towns that refused to hear Christ would experience something worse. The level of punishment in hell seems to be tied to the amount of light a person rejects.

Another indication that hell has different levels of punishment is found in Jesus' words in Luke 12: "The servant who knows the master's will and does not get ready or does not do what the master wants will be beaten with many blows. But the one who does not know and does things deserving punishment will be beaten with few blows. From everyone who has been given much, much will be demanded; and from the one who has been entrusted with much, much more will be asked" (verses 47–48).

Whatever degrees of punishment hell contains, it is clear that hell is a place to be avoided.

Unfortunately, the Bible states that most people will wind up in hell: "Wide is the gate and broad is the road that leads to destruction, and many enter through it. But small is the gate and narrow the road that leads to life, and only a few find it" (Matthew 7:13–14). The question one must ask is "which road am I on?" The "many" on the broad road have one thing in common—they have all rejected Christ as the one and only way to heaven. Jesus said, "I am the way and the truth and the life. No one comes to the Father except through me" (John 14:6). When He said He is the only way, that is precisely what He meant. Everyone following another "way" besides Jesus Christ is on the broad road to destruction, and the suffering is hideous, dreadful, eternal, and unavoidable.

77. If God is omnipresent, does that mean God is in hell?

God's omnipresence is one of His essential attributes. His justice is also essential, and, therefore, it is necessary for Him to punish unrepentant sinners. Hell is described as a place where people are removed from God's presence (see Matthew 25:41), yet God is everywhere present. This is a paradox.

Three passages are particularly important to this discussion. First is Psalm 139:7–8, in which David says, "Where can I go from Your Spirit? Or where can I flee from Your presence? If I ascend into heaven, You are there; If I make my bed in hell, behold, You are there" (NKJV). The word translated "hell" in the NKJV is the Hebrew *Sheol,* which simply means "the grave" or "the place of the dead." *Sheol* is a broad term and is not synonymous with *hell,* a word commonly used to refer to the eternal place of punishment.

All Psalm 139 says is that God is as present in the afterlife as He is in this life.

Second Thessalonians 1:9 says that those who do not know God "will suffer the punishment of eternal destruction, *away from the presence of the Lord* and from the glory of his might" (ESV, emphasis added). Compare this to Revelation 14:10, which says that people who worship the Antichrist "will be tormented with burning sulfur *in the presence of the holy angels and of the Lamb*" (emphasis added). These two verses delineate the apparent contradiction. But there is a rather simple explanation to be found in the original Greek.

In Revelation 14:10, "presence" is a literal translation of the Greek *enopion*, which means "in the presence of, before." This is a spatial word, suggesting proximity and literal, measurable distances. In contrast, the word translated "presence" in 2 Thessalonians is *prosopon*, which most commonly refers to a person's face or outward appearance. Paul in 2 Thessalonians appears to have taken this verbiage directly from Isaiah 2:10 as found in the Septuagint. There are other references to God and His people being "separated," even on earth (see Psalm 22:1). Theologian Dr. Louis Berkhof teaches that Paul refers to "a total absence of the favor of God."[15] This description of hell would present a more exact opposite to heaven. Heaven provides blessing and wholeness not through being closer *spatially* to God, but by being in complete fellowship with Him. Hell is associated with a complete lack of blessing due to the severing of any fellowship with God.

In heaven, believers will "see his face" (Revelation 22:4). At that moment, they will behold all of God's beauty, grace, and perfection. In hell, sinners will know nothing of beauty, grace, or perfection, as God, as it were, turns His face away.

Ultimately, it appears that God is indeed "present" in hell, or hell is in His presence, depending on how one looks at it. God is and will forever be omnipresent. He will forever know what is happening in hell. However, this does not mean that the souls imprisoned there will have a relationship with God or engage in communication with Him. He will be spatially present but relationally distant.

78. What kind of bodies will people have in hell?

The Bible indicates that both believers and nonbelievers will have resurrected bodies on the last day (Daniel 12:1–2). Those going to hell will be eternally separated from God. That's the "second death"—being cast into the lake of fire to be tormented for eternity, separated from God (Revelation 20:14).

One clue that people in hell have a body of some kind is Jesus' account of the rich man and Lazarus in Luke 16. The rich man in hell had the ability to feel "torment" and "agony," the ability to see and speak, and a "tongue" that he wanted cooled (verses 23–25). Since this story is set before the resurrection on the last day, it seems that those now in hell exist in an "intermediate" state; many theologians believe this to include a "spiritual body" of some type—or perhaps the spirit takes on some of the attributes of the body it inhabited.

People currently in heaven also have a "spiritual body," it would seem. Lazarus's "finger" is mentioned in Luke 16:24. And, when the three disciples saw Moses and Elijah on the mount of transfiguration, the two prophets did not appear as disembodied spirits; rather, they were recognizable individuals. They were visible as "men . . . in glorious splendor" (Luke 9:30). Even pre-resurrection, Moses and Elijah have a body of some kind.

Another indication that people will have physical bodies in hell is that Jesus warned us to "fear him who can destroy both soul and body in hell" (Matthew 10:28 ESV). The eternal, continuing destruction of hell is the product of God's justice and wrath, and the destruction of that place will affect the "body" as well as the soul.

The problem some people have with the concept of having a physical body in hell is that, if the fire of hell is literal, one's bodily tissue would be perpetually burning and regenerating to be burned again. But Scripture teaches that the resurrection body will be different from the bodies we now possess. Our earthly bodies are fit for this world; the resurrection body will be fit for eternity—in either heaven or hell.

God has good news regarding the harsh reality of hell's existence. God, in His justice, prepared hell for the punishment of sin; but, in His mercy, He also provided the means for us to be saved. Romans 5:8–9 states, "God demonstrates his own love for us in this: While we were still sinners, Christ died for us. Since we have now been justified by his blood, how much more shall we be saved from God's wrath through him!" Because of Christ's sacrifice and our faith in His atoning blood, we can be at peace with God (Romans 5:1). We can look forward to the time when we will live with Him for all eternity in the resurrected bodies He will give us.

What a blessing it is to be at peace with God. What a privilege to be called His child, His friend. We can enjoy the peace and joy of His presence both now and forever.

79. Is Satan the master of hell? Do Satan and his demons punish people in hell?

There is a common misconception that Satan is in charge of hell and that he and his demons live there and use their pitchforks to torment souls for eternity. This concept has no basis in Scripture whatsoever. In fact, Satan will be one of the tormented in the lake of fire, not the tormentor (Revelation 20:10).

Where does the idea that Satan is the master of hell come from, if not from the Bible? Much of the false thinking may come from Dante Alighieri's *The Divine Comedy* and John Milton's *Paradise Lost*. Many other works of art, and literary pieces such as Dan

Brown's novel *Inferno*, follow Dante's lead and picture Satan as the one in charge of hell.

Dante's poem describes the brutal descent of sinners into the underworld. Dante journeys through different levels of hell and purgatory and eventually arrives in paradise. The poem itself was an amalgamation of myths, Catholic ideas (like purgatory), and Islamic traditions about Muhammad's "night of ascension" (*lailat al-miraj*). Dante's medieval view of hell is influenced more by the Qur'an than the Bible.

Dante's literary vision of hell is depicted by Botticelli in his painting *Map of Hell* as a subterranean funnel of suffering—a wretched underground landscape of fire, brimstone, sewage, and monsters, with Satan himself waiting at its core. It's all very disturbing, and effective as a work of art, but it is based on the imaginations of men, not the Word of God.

Satan is not the ruler of hell. It is God who is in charge. Jesus says, "Do not be afraid of those who kill the body and after that can do no more. . . . Fear him who, after your body has been killed, has authority to throw you into hell. Yes, I tell you, fear him" (Luke 12:4–5). Jesus is referring to God here. He alone has the power to throw someone into hell. Who holds the keys of death and Hades? Jesus has absolute control over that domain (Revelation 1:18).

The lake of fire, mentioned only in Revelation 19:20 and 20:10, 14–15, is the final place of punishment for all unrepentant rebels, both angelic and human (Matthew 25:41). The universal punishment for all who reject Jesus Christ as Savior is to be "thrown into the lake of fire" (Revelation 20:15). The Bible speaks of hell as a place of "outer darkness" where there will be "weeping and gnashing of teeth" (Matthew 8:12; 22:13 ESV). Those whose names are written in the Lamb's Book of Life should have no fear of this terrible fate. By faith in Christ and His shed blood, we are destined to live eternally in the presence of God.

Satan does not rule hell or lead his demons in tormenting those who are banished there. In fact, the Bible does not say that Satan has been to hell yet. Rather, "eternal fire" is awaiting Satan; the place was originally created to punish Satan and the demons (Matthew 25:41), not to give them a kingdom to rule.

Until Satan is condemned and thrown into the pit forever, he spends his time between heaven (Job 1:6–12) and earth (1 Peter 5:8). He will not always have freedom of movement, and he knows it. "Woe to the earth and the sea, because the devil has gone down to you! He is filled with fury, because he knows that his time is short" (Revelation 12:12).

80. Is hell real? Is hell eternal?

It is interesting that a much higher percentage of people believe in the existence of heaven than believe in the existence of hell. According to the Bible, though, hell is just as real as heaven. The Bible explicitly teaches that hell is a real place to which the wicked/unbelieving are sent after death. We have all sinned against God (Romans 3:23). The just punishment for sin is death (Romans 6:23). Since all our sin is ultimately against God (Psalm 51:4), and since God is infinitely glorious, the punishment for sin must also be infinite. Eternal hell—the second death—is the punishment we have earned because of our sin.

The reality of hell was taught by Jesus. His warnings about hell are unambiguous in passages such as Matthew 5:22; Mark 9:47–48; and Luke 12:5. Pastor Alistair Begg draws this conclusion: "Is Jesus Christ true in what He says? And if we start from that premise, then we simply can't excise the hard parts out of it. We've got to take Him at His word. So that the most loving person who has ever lived spoke so straightforwardly about the awfulness of hell."[16]

The punishment of the wicked dead in hell is described in Scripture as "eternal fire" (Matthew 25:41), "unquenchable fire" (Matthew 3:12), "shame and everlasting contempt" (Daniel 12:2), a place where "the fire is not quenched" (Mark 9:48), a place of "torment" and "fire" (Luke 16:23–24), "everlasting destruction" (2 Thessalonians 1:9), a place of "burning sulfur" where "the smoke of . . . torment will rise for ever and ever" (Revelation 14:10–11), and a "lake of burning sulfur" where the wicked are "tormented day and night for ever and ever" (Revelation 20:10).

The punishment of the wicked in hell is as never-ending as the bliss of the righteous in heaven. Jesus Himself indicates that punishment in hell is just as everlasting as life in heaven (Matthew 25:46). The wicked are forever subject to the fury and the wrath of God. Those in hell will acknowledge the perfect justice of God and the lordship of Jesus Christ, the Savior they rejected (Psalm 76:10; Philippians 2:10–11).

Yes, hell is real. Yes, hell is a place of torment and punishment that lasts forever and ever, with no end. Praise God that, through Jesus, we can escape this eternal fate (John 3:16, 18, 36).

SECTION 9

Questions about Judgment and Eternity

81. When will the resurrection take place?

The Bible is clear that resurrection is a reality and that this life is not all that there is. While death is the end of physical life, it is not the end of human existence. Many believe in one general resurrection at the end of the age, but the Bible teaches that there will be not one resurrection but a series of resurrections, some to eternal life in heaven and some to eternal damnation (Daniel 12:2; John 5:28–29).

The first great resurrection was the resurrection of Jesus Christ. It is documented in each of the four Gospels (Matthew 28; Mark 16; Luke 24; John 20), cited several times in Acts (Acts 1:22; 2:31; 4:2, 33; 26:23), and mentioned repeatedly in the letters to the churches (Romans 1:4; Philippians 3:10; 1 Peter 1:3). Much is made of the importance of Christ's resurrection in 1 Corinthians 15:5–28, which records that over five hundred people saw Him at one of His post-resurrection appearances. Christ's resurrection is the "firstfruits" or guarantee to every Christian that he will also be resurrected. Christ's resurrection is also the basis of the Christian's certainty that all people who have died will one day be raised to face fair and even-handed judgment by Jesus Christ (Acts 17:30–31). The resurrection to eternal life is described as "the first resurrection" (Revelation 20:5–6); the resurrection to judgment and torment will be followed by "the second death" (Revelation 20:6, 13–15).

The first great resurrection of the church will occur at the time of the rapture. All those who have placed their trust in Jesus Christ during the church age and have died before Jesus returns will be resurrected at the rapture. The church age began on the day of Pentecost and will end when Christ returns to take believers back to heaven with Him (John 14:1–3; 1 Thessalonians 4:16–17). The apostle Paul explained that not all Christians will die, but all will be changed, i.e., given resurrection-type bodies (1 Corinthians 15:50–58), some without having to die. Christians who are alive and those who have already died will be caught up to meet the Lord in the air and be with Him always.

Another great resurrection will occur when Christ returns to earth (His second coming) at the end of the tribulation period. After the rapture, which closes the church age, the tribulation is the next event in God's chronology. This will be a time of terrible judgment upon the world, described in detail in Revelation chapters 6–18. Though all church age believers will be gone, millions of people left behind on earth will come to their senses during this time and will trust in Jesus as their Savior. Tragically, most of them will pay for their faith in Jesus by losing their lives (Revelation 6:9–11; 7:9–17; 13:7, 15–17; 17:6; 19:1–2). These believers in Jesus who die during the tribulation will be resurrected at Christ's return to reign with Him for a thousand years (Revelation

20:4, 6). Old Testament believers such as Job, Noah, Abraham, David, and even John the Baptist (who was assassinated before the church began) will be resurrected at this time also. Several passages in the Old Testament mention this event (Job 19:25–27; Isaiah 26:19; Daniel 12:1–2; Hosea 13:14). Ezekiel 37:1–14 describes the regathering of the nation of Israel using the symbolism of dead corpses coming back to life. But, given the language used, a physical resurrection of dead Israelites cannot be excluded from the passage. Again, all believers in God (in the Old Testament era) and all believers in Jesus (in the New Testament era) participate in the first resurrection, a resurrection to life (Revelation 20:4, 6).

There may be another resurrection at the end of the millennium; it is implied in Scripture, never explicitly taught. It is possible that some believers will die a physical death during the millennium. Through the prophet Isaiah, God said, "Never again will there be in it an infant who lives but a few days, or an old man who does not live out his years; the one who dies at a hundred will be thought a mere child; the one who fails to reach a hundred will be considered accursed" (Isaiah 65:20). On the other hand, it is also possible that death in the millennium will only come to the disobedient. In either case, some kind of transformation will be required to fit believers' bodies in the millennium for a pristine existence.

One day, after the final judgment, God will destroy the entire universe, including the earth, with fire (2 Peter 3:7–12). This will be necessary to purge God's creation of its endemic evil and decay brought upon it by man's sin. In its place God will create a new heaven and a new earth (2 Peter 3:13; Revelation 21:1–4). But what will happen to those believers who survived the tribulation and entered the millennium in their natural bodies? And what will happen to those who were born during the millennium, trusted in Jesus, and continued to live in their natural bodies? Paul taught that flesh and blood, which is mortal and subject to decay, cannot inherit the kingdom of God. That eternal kingdom is inhabitable only by those with resurrected, glorified bodies that are immune to decay (1 Corinthians 15:35–49). Presumably, these believers will be given resurrection bodies without having to die. Precisely when this happens is not explained, but, logically, it must happen somewhere in the transition from the old earth to the new earth.

There is a final resurrection, apparently of all the unbelieving dead of all ages. Jesus Christ will raise them from the dead (John 5:25–29) after the millennium, the thousand-year reign of Christ (Revelation 20:5). This is the resurrection described by Daniel as an awakening from "the dust of the earth . . . to shame and everlasting contempt" (Daniel 12:2). It is described by Jesus as a resurrection of judgment (John 5:28–29).

The apostle John saw a "great white throne" set up to judge the wicked (Revelation 20:11). Heaven and earth fled away from the One sitting on it, seeking a place to hide from His wrath. All the (godless) dead will stand before the throne. They, too, will possess resurrection-type bodies that can feel pain but will never cease to exist (Mark 9:43–48). They will be judged, and their punishment will be commensurate with their works. But there is another book opened—the Lamb's Book of Life (Revelation 21:27). Those whose names are not written in the book of life are cast into the "lake of fire," which amounts to "the second death" (Revelation 20:11–15). No indication is given that any names of those who appear at this judgment *are* found in the book of life. Rather, the book of life contains the names of the blessed—those who received forgiveness and partook of the first resurrection, the resurrection to life (Revelation 20:6).

82. What is eternal death?

Eternal death is the fate that awaits all people who ultimately reject God, reject the gospel of His Son, Jesus Christ, and remain in their sin and disobedience. Physical death is a one-time experience.

Eternal death, on the other hand, is everlasting. It is a death that continues through eternity, a spiritual death that involves a separation from God. Just as spiritual life, by grace through faith in Christ (Ephesians 2:8–9), is everlasting, eternal death is never-ending.

Does the Bible teach the doctrine of eternal death? Yes, the Bible clearly teaches an eternal separation of the wicked from God. Here are three passages, one from the Old Testament and two from the New, that support the doctrine of eternal death:

- "And many of those who sleep in the dust of the earth shall awake, some to everlasting life, and some to shame and everlasting contempt" (Daniel 12:2 ESV).
- "And [the wicked] will go away into eternal punishment, but the righteous into eternal life" (Matthew 25:46 ESV).
- "Then Death and Hades were thrown into the lake of fire. This is the second death, the lake of fire. And if anyone's name was not found written in the book of life, he was thrown into the lake of fire" (Revelation 20:14–15 ESV). Verse 10 emphasizes the perpetual state of torment associated with eternal death, as the lake of fire burns "forever and ever."

All three of these passages (and more could be added) have as their main context the scene of final judgment. After Jesus Christ returns, three things will occur:

1) The general resurrection
2) The final judgment
3) The inauguration of the eternal state

The fate of the righteous and the wicked could not be more different. The righteous—who are declared righteous on the merits of their Savior, Jesus Christ—will be ushered into a final state of glory. Meanwhile, the wicked—who have rejected Christ—will be sent to the lake of fire for eternal punishment and torment. Note too (particularly in the Daniel and Matthew passages) that the same adjective (*everlasting* or *eternal*) is used to modify both *life* and *punishment/contempt*. Both the life and the punishment last forever.

The doctrine of eternal death is not a popular one. However, truth is independent of the popular vote. The truth is that, due to our sin, we are under the just condemnation of God. God has sent His Son to die in our place and rise again to reconcile us to God. We can choose to embrace the saving message of Jesus Christ and have forgiveness and eternal life. Or we can decide we don't need the Son of God, in which case we will perish in our sin and be under God's judgment. To reject the Source of life is to choose eternal death.

83. What does the Bible say about when God will judge us?

There are two separate judgments, one for believers and one for unbelievers. One is a judgment that does not lead to condemnation (Romans 8:1); the other judgment will result in eternal condemnation (Revelation 20:15).

Believers are judged at the judgment seat of Christ (Romans 14:10–12). We believe that this judgment will probably occur in heaven during the seven-year tribulation on earth. Every believer will give an account of himself before the Lord. This judgment does not determine salvation, which is by faith alone (Ephesians 2:8–9); rather, it determines the rewards believers will receive.

First Corinthians 3:11 pictures Christ as our "foundation," and the surrounding verses liken the Christian life to building on that foundation. We can build with "gold, silver, costly stones," or we can build with "wood, hay or straw" (verse 12). What we construct will be tested, as it were, by fire. Our worthless, shallow activity will not survive God's refining fire; only what is done for God's glory will last. The judgment seat of Christ will reveal this.

Believers will be rewarded based on their good works in Christ's service and their faithfulness to the Lord (cf. 1 Corinthians 9:24–27). We will give an account of our actions, inactions, words, thoughts, and motives. Were they truly indicative of our position in Christ? "So then, each of us will give an account of ourselves to God" (Romans 14:12).

The second judgment is that of unbelievers. This will occur at the end of time, after the millennium and the final rebellion of Satan on earth. This judgment of the wicked is called the great white throne judgment (Revelation 20:11–15). This judgment does not determine salvation, either. Everyone at the great white throne is an unbeliever who has rejected Christ in life, and his fate is already sealed. Revelation 20:12 says that unbelievers will be "judged according to what they had done as recorded in the books." Those who have rejected Christ as Lord and Savior will be judged based on their works alone, and no human work can atone for sin or earn salvation: "By the works of the law no one will be justified" (Galatians 2:16). All their thoughts, words, and actions will be measured against God's perfect standard, and they will be found wanting. There will be no reward for the unbelieving, only eternal condemnation and punishment.

In summary, after death (or the rapture), believers in Christ will stand before the Lord to give an account. They will be judged on the basis of Christ's perfect, praiseworthy work on their behalf. After death, unbelievers will also stand before the Lord, who will examine their records. They will be judged on the basis of their own imperfect, unworthy work and their rejection of Christ's word (John 12:48).

84. What is the judgment seat of Christ?

Scripture gives us a reason not to judge one another: "For we will all stand before the judgment seat of God. . . . So then each of us will give an account of himself to God" (Romans 14:10–12 ESV). None of us are qualified to be the Judge. Only the Lord Jesus is qualified, and all judgment has been entrusted to Him (John 5:22). We will all stand someday before the judgment seat of Christ.

The judgment seat of Christ involves a time in the future when believers will give an account of themselves to Christ. This is the plain teaching of Scripture: "We must all appear before the judgment seat of Christ, so that each of us may receive what is due us for the things done while in the body, whether good or bad" (2 Corinthians 5:10). The warning is to Christians, not unbelievers. As Jesus taught in His parable, the king is going to return, at which time he will require an account from his servants (Luke 19:11–26).

The judgment seat of Christ is different from the great white throne judgment. That will be the final judgment of the wicked prior to their being cast into the lake of fire (Revelation 20:11–15). Appearing before the great white throne will be unbelievers. Believers will appear before the judgment seat of Christ.

The judgment seat of Christ does *not* determine our salvation; that matter was settled by Christ's sacrifice on our behalf (1 John 2:2) and our faith in Him (John 3:16). All our sins are forgiven, and there is "no condemnation for those who are in Christ Jesus" (Romans 8:1). Jesus said, "Very truly I tell you, whoever hears my word and believes him who sent me has eternal life and *will not be judged* but has crossed over from death to life" (John 5:24, emphasis added).

So, believers are secure in Christ, but they still must appear before the judgment seat of Christ. It will be a time of examination and a time of reward. Jesus will inspect our works. What did we do with the resources God gave us? How faithful were we? Were we yielded to the Spirit, seeking to honor Christ and further His work in the world? If so, we will have reward (see Matthew 10:41–42). Did we neglect our opportunities to serve the Lord? If so, we will suffer loss of reward. Paul likens our Christian service to erecting a building:

Each one should build with care. For no one can lay any foundation other than the one already laid, which is Jesus Christ. If anyone builds on this foundation using gold, silver, costly stones, wood, hay or straw, their work will be shown for what it is, because the Day will bring it to light. It will be revealed with fire, and the fire will test the quality of each person's work. If what has been built survives, the builder will receive a reward. If it is burned up, the builder will suffer loss but yet will be saved—even though only as one escaping through the flames.

1 Corinthians 3:10–15

Note, in the above passage, our works subsequent to Christ's salvation are of two different types—good and bad. The "fire" of God's scrutiny will reveal the quality of our works. As Arthur Pink points out, "'Gold, silver, precious stones' are of *intrinsic* value, whereas 'wood, hay, stubble' are a *natural* growth."[17] Rewards are distributed to those whose works withstand the test. Those whose works have a natural source will "suffer loss." Their works will be burned up, but they themselves "will be saved." The judgment seat of Christ, then, does not confer or rescind salvation.

The judgment seat of Christ is also not a time to punish sin. Jesus took our punishment once and for all. The judgment seat of Christ is a time when we will be called on to report, to render an accounting of what we did for Jesus. It will be a serious and necessary time of reckoning, but, as God's redeemed, we will never be condemned with the wicked. As one theologian put it, "It cannot be too strongly emphasized that the judgment is unrelated to the problem of sin, that it is more for the bestowing of rewards than the rejection of failure."[18]

In the Greek, a single word is used for "judgment seat" in Romans 14:10 and 2 Corinthians 5:10—the word is *bema*. A *bema* was a raised platform on which judges sat to view athletic games. Their job was to make sure contestants followed the rules and to present awards to the victors (see 1 Corinthians 9:24–27). The *bema* was never a place to reprimand the athletes or to punish them in any way. It was a place of testing and reward. In the same way, the *bema* of Christ will not be a place of condemnation or censure.

In anticipation of the judgment seat of Christ, we are careful in what we say and do in this life. James gives this advice: "Speak and act as those who are going to be judged by the law that gives freedom" (James 2:12; cf. Matthew 12:36). We want to give our account with joy on that day, and that is why we strive to serve the Lord faithfully today.

The Bible speaks of believers receiving crowns for different things. The various crowns are described in 2 Timothy 2:5; 4:8; James 1:12; 1 Peter 5:4; and Revelation 2:10. We believe the judgment seat of Christ is when the crowns will be awarded, and this will take place in heaven soon after the rapture of the church (as described in 1 Thessalonians 4:13–18).

At the very end of the Bible, Jesus said, "Look, I am coming soon! My reward is with me, and I will give to each person according to what they have done" (Revelation 22:12). In preparation for the judgment seat of Christ, what are you choosing to "build" with? Gold, silver, and precious stones—things that will last? Or wood, hay, and straw—things that will not stand the day of testing?

85. What is the purpose of there being rewards in heaven?

The Bible mentions rewards in heaven multiple times (Matthew 5:12; Luke 6:23, 35; 1 Corinthians 3:14; 9:18). But why are rewards necessary? Won't being in heaven with God be enough? Experiencing Him, His glory, and the joys of heaven will be so wonderful, it's hard to understand why extra rewards would be needed. Also, since our faith rests in Christ's righteousness instead of our own (Romans 3:21–26), it seems strange that our works would merit reward.

God will give rewards in heaven at the *bema*, or the judgment seat of Christ, based on our faithfulness in service to Him (2 Corinthians 5:10). The rewards will show the reality of our sonship (Galatians 4:7) and the justice of God (Hebrews 6:10). God will give rewards in heaven in order to fulfill the law of sowing and reaping (Galatians 6:7–9) and make good on His promise that our labor in the Lord is not in vain (1 Corinthians 15:58).

One reason for the rewards in heaven is the fact that Jesus shares His reward with us. Paul said, "I no longer live, but Christ lives in me. The life I now live in the body, I live by faith in the Son of God, who loved me and gave himself for me" (Galatians 2:20). Our lives are "hidden" with Christ, who is seated at the right hand of God (Colossians 3:1–4). We die with Him and we live with Him and we share in His joy (Romans 6:8; Matthew 25:21). In heaven we will dwell with Him (John 14:1–3). Our lives are inextricably linked with Christ's. The reward He receives is shared with all of us: "If we are children, then we are heirs—heirs of God and co-heirs with Christ, if indeed we share in his sufferings in order that we may also share in his glory" (Romans 8:17).

Our rewards in heaven depend on the goodness and power of God. Through Christ's resurrection we gain an inheritance in heaven; on earth our faith is tested and results in praise and glory and honor when Christ is revealed (1 Peter 1:3–9). The things we do in this life are only permanent (that is, carried with us into heaven) if they are built on the foundation, which is Christ (1 Corinthians 3:11–15).

The rewards we gain in heaven are not like the rewards we earn here on earth. We tend to think in material terms—mansions, jewels, etc. But these things are only representations of the true rewards we will gain in heaven. A child who wins a spelling bee treasures the trophy he receives not for the sake of the trophy itself but for what that trophy means. Likewise, any rewards or honor we gain in heaven will be precious to us because they carry the weight and meaning of our relationship with God—and because they remind us of what He did through us on earth.

In this way, rewards in heaven glorify God and provide us with joy, peace, and wonder as we consider God's work in us and through us. The closer we were to God during this life, the more centered on Him and aware of Him, the more dependent on Him, the more desperate for His mercy, the more there will be to celebrate. We are like characters in a story who suffer doubt, loss, and fear, wondering if we will ever really have our heart's desire. When the happy ending comes and desire is fulfilled, there comes a completion. The story would not be satisfying without that completion. Rewards in heaven are the completion of our earthly story, and those rewards will be eternally satisfying (Psalm 16:11).

86. What happens at the final judgment?

The first thing to understand about the final judgment is that it cannot be avoided. Regardless of how we may choose to interpret prophecy on the end times, "people are destined to die once, and after that to face judgment" (Hebrews 9:27). We all have a divine appointment with our Creator. The apostle John recorded some details of the final judgment:

> Then I saw a great white throne and him who was seated on it. The earth and the heavens fled from his presence, and there was no place for them. And I saw the dead, great and small, standing before the throne, and books were opened. Another book was opened, which is the book of life. The dead were judged according to what they had done as recorded in the books. The sea gave up the dead that were in it, and death and Hades gave up the dead that were in them, and each person was judged according to what they had done. Then death and Hades were thrown into the lake of fire. The lake of fire

is the second death. Anyone whose name was not found written in the book of life was thrown into the lake of fire.

Revelation 20:11–15

This remarkable passage describes the final judgment—the end of history and the beginning of the eternal state. We can be sure of this: no mistakes will be made in our hearings, as judgment is meted out by the perfect and all-knowing God (Matthew 5:48; 1 John 1:5). God will be perfectly just and fair (Acts 10:34; Galatians 3:28). God cannot be deceived or misled (Galatians 6:7). God is incorruptible and cannot be swayed by any prejudices, excuses, or lies (Luke 14:16–24).

As God the Son, Jesus Christ will be the judge at the final judgment (John 5:22). All unbelievers will stand before Christ at the great white throne, and they will be punished according to the works they have done. The Bible says that unbelievers are currently storing up wrath against themselves (Romans 2:5) and that "God 'will repay each person according to what they have done'" (Romans 2:6). (Believers will be judged separately at the judgment seat of Christ, a judgment of examination and reward.) At the great white throne, the fate of the unsaved will be in the hands of the omniscient God, who will judge everyone according to his or her soul's condition and the works done in the body.

For now, our fate is in our own hands. The end of our soul's journey will either be in an eternal heaven or in an eternal hell (Matthew 25:46). We must choose our destination by either accepting or rejecting the sacrifice of Christ on our behalf. Further, we must make that choice before our physical lives come to an end. After we die, we no longer have a choice.

Everyone who has ever lived will face God someday. "Nothing in all creation is hidden from God's sight. Everything is uncovered and laid bare before the eyes of him to whom we must give account" (Hebrews 4:13).

87. What is the second death?

The second death is mentioned on multiple occasions in the book of Revelation and is synonymous with the lake of fire. It is a "death" in that it is a separation from God, the Giver of life. It is called the "second" one because it follows physical death.

Revelation 21:8 explains the second death in the most detail: "The cowardly, the unbelieving, the vile, the murderers, the sexually immoral, those who practice magic arts, the idolaters and all liars—they will be consigned to the fiery lake of burning sulfur. This is the second death."

Three other places in Revelation also mention the second death. The first is Revelation 2:11: "He who has an ear, let him hear what the Spirit says to the churches. The one who conquers will not be hurt by the second death" (ESV). In this verse, Jesus promises that believers will not experience the lake of fire (cf. 1 John 5:4). The second death is exclusively for those who have rejected Christ. It is not a place believers in Christ should fear.

Revelation 20:6 speaks of the second death in relation to a future period called the millennium: "Blessed and holy are those who share in the first resurrection. The second death has no power over them, but they will be priests of God and of Christ and will reign with him for a thousand years." This verse notes three important facts. First, those who die for their faith in Jesus during the tribulation will be resurrected to enter the millennium and live with Him. Second, these martyrs will escape the lake of fire or second death. Third, they will reign with Christ.

The second death is also mentioned in Revelation 20:14–15: "Then death and Hades were thrown into the lake of fire. The lake of fire is the second death. Anyone whose name was not found written in the book of life was thrown into the lake of fire." At the end of time, even death and the grave (Hades) will be thrown into the lake of fire. In addition, every person not included in the book of life will be thrown into the lake of fire. This condition will be final; the destination is permanent.

In summary, the second death is a reference to the lake of fire, where those who are separated from God by their sin will dwell for eternity. This judgment is recorded in Scripture as a warning to unbelievers to seek the salvation that Jesus Christ provides. The coming judgment should also challenge believers to share their faith. There is a vast difference between the final destination of those who know Christ and those who do not.

88. What are the new heaven and the new earth?

In Revelation 21:1, John sees something spectacular: "Then I saw 'a new heaven and a new earth,' for the first heaven and the first earth had passed away." This new earth and new heaven are sometimes referred to as the "eternal state." As seen in Revelation chapters 21–22, the new earth will be the eternal dwelling place of believers in Jesus Christ. Scripture gives us a few details of the new heaven and new earth.

The current heaven and earth have long been subject to God's curse because of mankind's sin. All creation "has been groaning as in the pains of childbirth" (Romans 8:22) as it awaits the fulfillment of God's plan and "the children of God to be revealed" (verse 19). "Heaven and earth will pass away" (Mark 13:31), and they will be replaced by the new heaven and the new earth. At that time, the Lord, seated on His throne, says, "I am making everything new!" (Revelation 21:5). In the new creation, sin will be totally eradicated, and "there shall be no more curse" (Revelation 22:3 NKJV).

The new heaven and new earth are also mentioned in Isaiah 65:17; 66:22; and 2 Peter 3:13. Peter says that the new heaven and new earth will be "where righteousness dwells." Isaiah says that "the former things will not be remembered, nor will they come to mind." Things will be completely new, and the old order of things, with the accompanying sorrow and tragedy, will be gone.

The new earth will be free from sin, evil, sickness, suffering, and death. It will be earth as God originally intended it to be, prior to the curse of sin. It will be Eden restored.

A major feature of the new earth will be the New Jerusalem. John calls it "the Holy City . . . coming down out of heaven from God, prepared as a bride beautifully dressed for her husband" (Revelation 21:2). This glorious city, with its streets of gold and pearly gates, is situated on a new, glorious earth. The tree of life will be there (Revelation 22:2). This city represents the final state of redeemed mankind, forever in fellowship with God: "God's dwelling place is now among the people, and he will dwell with them. They will be his people, and God himself will be with them and be their God. . . . His servants will serve him. They will see his face" (Revelation 21:3; 22:3–4).

In the new heaven and new earth, Scripture says, there are seven things notable for their absence—seven things that are "no more":

- no more sea (Revelation 21:1)
- no more death (Revelation 21:4)
- no more mourning (Revelation 21:4)
- no more weeping (Revelation 21:4)
- no more pain (Revelation 21:4)
- no more curse (Revelation 22:3)
- no more night (Revelation 22:5)

The creation of the new heaven and new earth brings the promise that God "will wipe every tear from their eyes" (Revelation 21:4). This event comes *after* the tribulation, *after* the Lord's second coming, *after* the millennial kingdom, *after* the final rebellion, *after* the final judgment of Satan, and *after* the great white throne judgment. The brief description of the new heaven and new earth is the last glimpse into eternity that the Bible gives.

89. What is the New Jerusalem?

The New Jerusalem, which is also called the tabernacle of God, the Holy City, the city of God, the Celestial City, the city foursquare, and heavenly Jerusalem, is literally heaven on earth. It is referred to in the Bible in several places (Galatians 4:26; Hebrews 11:10; 12:22–24; and 13:14), but it is most fully described in Revelation 21.

In Revelation 21, the recorded history of man is at its end. All the ages have come and gone. Christ has gathered His church in the rapture (1 Thessalonians 4:15–17). The tribulation has passed (Revelation 6–18). The battle of Armageddon has been fought and won by our Lord Jesus Christ (Revelation 19:17–21). Satan has been chained for the 1,000-year reign of Christ on earth (Revelation 20:1–3). A new, glorious temple has been established in Jerusalem (Ezekiel 40–48). The final rebellion against God has been quashed, and Satan has received his just punishment, an eternity in the lake of fire (Revelation 20:7–10.) The great white throne judgment has taken place, and mankind has been judged (Revelation 20:11–15).

In Revelation 21:1 God does a complete makeover of heaven and earth (cf. Isaiah 65:17; 2 Peter 3:12–13). The new heaven and new earth are what some call the eternal state and will be "where righteousness dwells" (2 Peter 3:13). After the re-creation, God reveals the New Jerusalem. John sees a glimpse of it in his vision: "The Holy City, the new Jerusalem, coming down out of heaven from God, prepared as a bride beautifully dressed for her husband" (Revelation 21:2). This is the city that Abraham looked for in faith (Hebrews 11:10). It is the place where God will dwell with His people forever (Revelation 21:3). Inhabitants of this celestial city will have all tears wiped away (Revelation 21:4).

The New Jerusalem will be fantastically huge. John records that the city is nearly 1,400 miles long, and it is as wide and as high as it is long—the New Jerusalem being equal in length, width, and depth (Revelation 21:15–17). The city will be dazzling in every way. It is lighted by the glory of God (verse 23). Its twelve foundations, bearing the names of the twelve apostles, are "decorated with every kind of precious stone" (verse 19). It has twelve gates, each made of a single pearl, bearing the names of the twelve tribes of Israel (verses 12 and 21). The street will be made of pure gold (verse 21).

The New Jerusalem will be a place of unimagined blessing. The curse of the old earth will be gone (Revelation 22:3). In the city are the tree of life "for the healing of the nations" and the river of life (verses 1–2). It is the place that Paul spoke of: "In the coming ages [God] might show the incomparable riches of his grace, expressed in his kindness to us in Christ Jesus" (Ephesians 2:7). The New Jerusalem is the ultimate fulfillment of all God's promises. The New Jerusalem is God's goodness made fully manifest.

Who are the residents of the New Jerusalem? The Father and the Lamb are there (Revelation 21:22). Angels are at the gates (verse 12). But the city will be filled with God's redeemed children. The New Jerusalem is the righteous counter to the evil Babylon (Revelation 17), destroyed by God's judgment (Revelation 18). The wicked had their city, and God has His.

To which city do you belong? Babylon the Great or the New Jerusalem? If you believe that Jesus, the Son of God, died and rose again and have asked God to save you by His grace, then you are a citizen of the New Jerusalem. "God raised [you] up with Christ and seated [you] with him in the heavenly realms in Christ Jesus" (Ephesians 2:6). You have "an inheritance that can never perish, spoil or fade" (1 Peter 1:4). If you have not yet trusted Christ as your Savior, then we urge you to receive Him. The invitation is extended: "The Spirit and the bride say, 'Come!' And let the one who hears say, 'Come!' Let the one who is thirsty come; and let the one who wishes take the free gift of the water of life" (Revelation 22:17).

90. Why will the nations need healing in the New Jerusalem?

One of God's promises concerning the eternal state is that the nations of the world will have healing. The question comes up, though, as to why exactly healing is needed. Isn't the New Jerusalem a place of perfection already?

The promise of the healing of the nations is found in Revelation 22, after the creation of the new heaven and new earth (Revelation 21:1). John writes,

> Then the angel showed me the river of the water of life, as clear as crystal, flowing from the throne of God and of the Lamb down the middle of the great street of the city. On each side of the river stood the tree of life, bearing twelve crops of fruit, yielding its fruit every month. And the leaves of the tree are for the healing of the nations. No longer will there be any curse. The throne of God and of the Lamb will be in the city, and his servants will serve him. They will see his face, and his name will be on their foreheads. There will be no more night. They will not need the light of a lamp or the light of the sun, for the Lord God will give them light. And they will reign for ever and ever.
>
> Revelation 22:1–5

The healing of the nations is linked to the tree of life, as God reestablishes Eden. It is the leaves of this tree that are said to be "for the healing of the nations" (Revelation 22:2). It is possible that the tree of life in the New Jerusalem is literal and that its leaves and various fruits will somehow enrich our existence in the eternal state. All the nations represented there will be "healed" of their divisions and strife in their equal access to the tree of life.

It is also possible that the tree of life in the New Jerusalem is symbolic and that its "healing" signifies the eternal life that all will enjoy there. The different fruits it bears could represent the unlimited variety of our existence in heaven. The clear flowing river that waters the tree could picture the spiritual life of God's redeemed—the "living water" Jesus promised in John 4:13–14.

The healing the tree of life's leaves provide is not the healing of the wounds of battle—warfare will have ended. The healing is not needed for combating sickness—there will be no more sickness, death, or pain (Revelation 21:4). No, the "healing" is a reference to the perpetual blessing of the new heaven and earth; never again will the world be plagued by physical disorders or spiritual malaise or corruption. There will be no more warfare, no strife, no conflicting factions. God will heal all that ails His creation, and there will be no more curse (Revelation 22:3).

In the eternal state, everything will be blessed, and the tree of life represents that blessedness. There will be perfect sinlessness, perfect government, perfect service to God, perfect communion, and perfect glory. It is impossible for us to imagine being totally separated from sin and living in a glorified state before God. But the Lord assures us that "these words are trustworthy and true" (Revelation 22:6).

SECTION 10

Questions about Alternate Afterlife Beliefs

91. How to get to heaven—what are the ideas from the different religions?

There appear to be five major categories regarding how to get to heaven in the world's religions. Most believe that hard work and wisdom will lead to ultimate fulfillment, whether that is unity with god (Hinduism, Buddhism, and Baha'i) or freedom and independence (Scientology, Jainism). Others, like Unitarianism and Wicca, teach the afterlife is whatever you want it to be, and salvation is a nonissue because the sin nature doesn't exist. A few believe either the afterlife doesn't exist or it's too unknowable to consider.

Derivatives of the worship of the Christian-Judeo God generally hold that faith in God and/or Jesus and the accomplishment of various deeds, including baptism or door-to-door evangelism, will ensure the worshiper will go to heaven. Only biblical Christianity teaches that salvation is a free gift of God through faith in Christ (Ephesians 2:8–9).

Here are various faith systems and what they teach about how to get to heaven:

Atheism: Most atheists believe there is no heaven—no afterlife at all. Upon death, people simply cease to exist. Others attempt to define the afterlife using quantum mechanics and other scientific methods.

Baha'i: Like many other religions, Baha'i doesn't teach that man was born with a sin nature or that man needs saving from evil. Man simply needs saving from his erroneous beliefs of how the world works and how he is to interact with the world. God sent messengers to explain to people how to come to this knowledge: Abraham, Krishna, Zoroaster, Moses, Buddha, Jesus, Muhammad, and Baha'u'llah. These prophets progressively revealed the nature of god to the world. Upon death, a person's soul continues its spiritual journey, perhaps through the states known as heaven and hell, until it comes to a final resting point, united with god.

Buddhism: Buddhism also believes that to reach heaven, or "nirvana," is to be rejoined in spirit with god. Nirvana is a transcendental, blissful spiritual state, and attaining it requires following the Eightfold Path. This includes understanding the universe and acting, speaking, and living in the right manner and with the right intentions. Mastering these and the other of the eight paths will return a worshiper's spirit to god.

Chinese Religion: Chinese religion is not an organized church, but an amalgamation of different religions and beliefs including Taoism and Buddhism. Upon death, worshipers are judged. The good are sent either to a Buddhist paradise or a Tao dwelling place. The bad are sent to hell for a period of time and then reincarnated.

Christianity: Christianity is the only religion that teaches man can do nothing to earn or pay his way into heaven. Man, a slave to the sin nature he was born with, must completely rely on the grace of God in applying Jesus Christ's sacrifice to himself. People are forgiven of sin and saved by faith in the death and resurrection of Christ. Upon death, the spirits of Christians go to heaven, while the spirits of unbelievers go to hell. At the final judgment, unbelievers are separated from God for eternity in the lake of fire.

Confucianism: Confucianism concentrates on appropriate behavior in life, not a future heaven. The afterlife is unknowable, so all effort should be concentrated on this life to make it the best it can be, to honor ancestors, and to respect elders.

Eastern Orthodoxy: Orthodoxy is a Christian-Judeo derivative that reinterprets key Scripture verses in such a way that works become essential to reach heaven. Orthodoxy teaches that faith in Jesus is necessary for salvation but is only a *part* of the salvation process. If that process (called *theosis*) is not performed appropriately, a worshiper can lose his or her salvation. After death, the devout live in an intermediate state where this *theosis* can be completed. Those who have belief but did not accomplish sufficient progress in *theosis* are sent to a temporary "direful condition" and will go to hell unless the devout on earth pray and complete acts of mercy on their behalf. After final judgment, the saved are sent to heaven and the others to hell. Heaven and hell are not locations, but reactions to being in the presence of God, as there is nowhere that He is not present. Everyone will experience the presence of God for eternity. Whether that experience is joyful or painful depends on the condition of one's heart. For Christ-followers, life after death will be the wonderful enjoyment of God's presence. For the faithless and unbelieving, life after death will consist of the supreme torture of His presence.

Hinduism: Hinduism is similar to Buddhism in some ways. Salvation (or *moksha*) is reached when the worshiper is freed from the cycle of reincarnation and his spirit becomes one with god. One becomes free by ridding oneself of bad karma—the effect of evil action or evil intent. This can be done in three different ways: through selfless devotion to and service of a particular god, through understanding the nature of the universe, or by mastering the actions needed to fully appease the gods. In Hinduism, with over a million different gods, there are differences of opinion regarding the nature of salvation. The Advaita school teaches that salvation occurs when one strips away the false self and makes the soul indistinguishable from that of god. The dualist insists that one's soul always retains its own identity even as it is joined with god.

Islam: Islam is a take-off on the Christian/Judeo God, but salvation is work-based and not by grace. Muslims believe salvation comes to those who obey Allah to the point that their good deeds outweigh their bad. Muslims hope that repeating what Muhammad did and said will be enough to get to heaven, but they also recite extra prayers, fast, go on pilgrimages, and perform good works in hope of tipping the scales. Martyrdom in service to Allah is the only work guaranteed to send a worshiper to paradise.

Jainism: Jainism came to be in India about the same time as Hinduism and is similar. One must hold the right belief, have the right knowledge, and act in the right manner. Only then can the soul be cleansed of bad karma. But in Jainism, there is no creator. There is no higher god to reach or lend aid. Salvation is seen as man being the master of his own destiny, liberated and perfect, filled with infinite perception, knowledge, bliss, and power.

Jehovah's Witnesses: The teachings of the Watchtower Society lead us to categorize the Jehovah's Witnesses as a cult of Christianity that denies the personality of the Holy Spirit and teaches that Christ is a created being. Similar to Mormons, Jehovah's Witnesses teach different levels of heaven. The anointed are 144,000 who receive salvation by the blood of Christ and will rule with Him in paradise. They are the bride of Christ. For all others, Jesus' sacrifice only freed them from Adam's curse of original sin, and "faith" is merely the opportunity to earn their way to heaven. The faithful must learn about Kingdom history, keep the laws of Jehovah, and be loyal to "God's government"—the 144,000 leaders, 9,000 of whom are currently on the earth. They must also spread the news about the Kingdom through door-to-door proselytizing and other means. Upon death, the faithful will be resurrected during the millennial kingdom and must continue a devout life. The righteous will live for eternity under the rule of the 144,000.

Judaism: Jews believe that, as individuals and as a nation, they can be reconciled to God. Through sin (individually or collectively) they can lose their salvation, but they can also earn it back through repentance, good deeds, and a life of devotion.

Mormonism: Mormons believe their religion to be a derivative of Judeo/Christianity, but their faulty view of Christ and their reliance on extra-grace works belies this. They also have a different view of heaven. To reach the second heaven under "general salvation," one must accept Christ (either in this life or the next) and be baptized or be baptized by proxy through a living relative. To reach the highest heaven, one must believe in God and Jesus, repent of sins, be baptized in the church, be a member of the LDS church, receive the Holy Ghost by the laying on of hands, obey the Mormon "Word of Wisdom" and all God's commandments, and complete certain temple rituals, including marriage. This "individual salvation" leads to the worshiper and his or her spouse becoming gods and giving birth to spirit children who return to earth as the souls of the living.

Roman Catholicism: Roman Catholics originally believed only those in the Roman Catholic Church could be saved. Joining the church was a long process of classes, rituals, and baptism. People who had already been baptized but were not members of the Roman Catholic Church faced different requirements and may even already be considered Christians. Baptism is "normatively" required for salvation, but this can include "baptism of blood" (i.e., martyrdom) or "baptism of desire" (wanting to be baptized). From the Catholic Catechism: "Those who die for the faith, those who are catechumens, and all those who, without knowing of the Church but acting under the inspiration of grace, seek God sincerely and strive to fulfill his will, are saved even if they have not been baptized."[19] Despite the changes through the years, baptism (or the desire for baptism) is still required for salvation.

According to Catholicism, upon death, the souls of those who rejected Christ are sent to hell. The souls of those who accepted Christ and performed sufficient acts to be purified of sin go to heaven. Those who died in faith but did not complete the steps to be purified are sent to purgatory, where they undergo temporary, painful punishment until their souls are cleansed. Purification by torment may be lessened by suffering during life and the offerings and prayers of others on the sinner's behalf. Once purification is complete, the soul may go to heaven.

Scientology: Scientology is similar to Eastern religions in that salvation is achieved through knowledge of self and the universe. The "thetan" (Scientology's answer to the soul) travels through several different lifetimes, attempting to expel painful and traumatic images that cause a person to act fearfully and irrationally. Once a Scientologist is "cleared" of these harmful images and becomes an "operating thetan," he or she is able to control thought, life, matter, energy, space, and time.

Shinto: The afterlife in Shinto was originally conceived as a dire, Hades-like realm. Matters of the afterlife have now been transferred to Buddhism. Salvation in Shinto is dependent on penance and avoiding impurity or pollution of the soul. Then one's soul can join those of its ancestors.

Sikhism: Sikhism was created in reaction to the conflict between Hinduism and Islam and shows influence from Hinduism— although Sikhs, like Muslims, are monotheistic. "Evil" is merely human selfishness. Salvation is attained by living an honest life and meditating on god. If good works are performed sufficiently, the worshiper is released from the cycle of reincarnation and becomes one with god.

Taoism: Like several other Eastern religions (Shinto, Chinese folk religions, Sikhism), Taoism adopted many of its afterlife principles from Buddhism. Initially, Taoists didn't concern themselves with worries of the afterlife and instead concentrated on creating a utopian society. Salvation was reached by aligning with the cosmos and receiving aid from supernatural immortals who resided on mountains, islands, and other earthly locales. The result was immortality. Eventually, Taoists abandoned the quest for immortality and adopted the afterlife teachings of Buddhism.

Unitarian-Universalism: Unitarians are allowed to and encouraged to believe anything they like about the afterlife and how to get there. In general, they believe people should seek enlightenment in this life and not worry too much about the afterlife.

Wicca: Wiccans believe many different things about the afterlife, but most seem to agree that there is no need for salvation. People either live in harmony with the goddess by caring for her physical manifestation—the earth—or they don't, and their bad karma is returned to them threefold. Some believe souls are reincarnated until they learn all their life lessons and become one with the goddess. Some are so committed to following one's individual path that they believe individuals determine what will happen when they die; if worshipers think they're going to be reincarnated or sent to hell or joined with the goddess, they will be. Others refuse to contemplate the afterlife at all. In any case, they don't believe in sin or anything they need saving from.

Zoroastrianism: Zoroastrianism may be the first religion that stated that the afterlife was dependent upon one's actions in life. There is no reincarnation, just a simple judgment four days after death. After a sufficient amount of time in hell, however, even the condemned can go to heaven. To be judged righteous, one can use knowledge or devotion, but the most effective way to righteousness is through action.

92. What do Jews believe about the afterlife?

Historically, there has been little unity of belief among Jewish people about any topic, including the topics of hell, eternal life, and final judgment. If you ask ten Jews about their beliefs on something, it is possible you will get ten different answers. Some Jews believe in hell, but most do not. Most Jews today have been more influenced by Eastern mysticism, secularism, and liberal theology than by the official tenets of Judaism. Another reason most Jewish people don't believe in hell is that Christianity teaches the doctrine of hell. Anything identified as "Christian thought" is often rejected outright as "not Jewish."

Belief in the eventual resurrection of the dead is a fundamental belief of traditional Judaism. But even that doctrine has been debated for centuries. A belief in resurrection distinguished the Pharisees (Rabbinical Judaism) from the Sadducees (see Acts 23:8). Divine reward and punishment are so basic to Judaism that they are taught in Maimonides' Thirteen Principles of the Jewish Faith. Denying hell is an example of the extent to which modern Jews have been influenced by secularism.

What a Jewish person believes about heaven and hell, known broadly as *Olam Ha-Ba* ("the World to Come"), depends on what he or she believes about God. Secular Jews, like secular Gentiles, usually believe that, at death, they just go into the ground and things are over. Jews with mystical leanings believe in reincarnation; others believe in resurrection.

Traditional Judaism teaches that after death our bodies go to the grave but our souls go before God to be judged. God, as Scripture states, is the only one who knows our motives as well as our works. God sees the heart, whereas man looks at the outside

(1 Samuel 16:7). Facing the only true Judge, we are assigned a place in heaven according to a merit system based on God's accounting of all our actions and motives. Traditional Jewish thought is that only the very righteous go directly to heaven; all others must be cleansed of residual sin.

According to traditional Judaism, sins that were not cleansed prior to death are removed after death in a place called Sheol or Gehinnom. The name of the place is taken from a valley (Gei Hinnom) just south of Jerusalem, once used for child sacrifice (2 Kings 23:10). Some Jews view Gehinnom as a place of torture and punishment, fire and brimstone. Others imagine it less harshly, as a place where one reviews the actions of his or her life and repents for past misdeeds. "Hell" in Judaism is a place where the soul is cleansed or refined (see Zechariah 13:9). The exceedingly righteous and those who repent before they die can avoid being "cleansed" in hell. This doctrine bears some similarity to the Catholic teaching of purgatory.

Contrary to the Christian view of eternal damnation in Hades or hell or the lake of fire, the "punishment" of Sheol, according to Judaism, is temporary. Judaism bases its doctrine of a temporary hell on Psalm 16:10, 1 Samuel 2:6, and Jonah 2:3. According to rabbinic teachings, the soul's sentence in Gehinnom is usually limited to a twelve-month period of purgatory before the soul takes its place in *Olam Ha-Ba*.[20] This twelve-month limit is reflected in the year-long mourning cycle and the recitation of the *kaddish*, the memorial prayer for the dead. Second Temple Judaism believed that, until the Messiah came, it was not possible for the faithful to enter heaven. The dead remained in Sheol, waiting.

In the Jewish view of hell, the pain the soul experiences is not physical; rather, it is psychological. The shame one feels upon reviewing one's personal history causes anguish, as does seeing how many opportunities to serve God were wasted. Almost everyone, including non-Jewish people, can merit a portion in the World to Come. But some will not be given a chance of heaven: "Multitudes who sleep in the dust of the earth will awake: some to everlasting life, others to shame and everlasting contempt" (Daniel 12:2). The "everlasting contempt," in the Jewish view, is reserved for completely evil, unredeemable people such as King Ahab, the men of Sodom, and Adolf Hitler.

Just as all Christians do not agree on eschatology, all Jewish people do not agree on the afterlife. What the Bible clearly teaches is that sin demands a price to be paid by someone, that Jesus paid that price for us, that there is an afterlife, and that, in Christ, both Jews and Gentiles can have a place of blessing in *Olam Ha-Ba*, the World to Come.

93. Is annihilationism biblical?

Annihilationism is the belief that unbelievers will not experience an eternity of suffering in hell but will instead be "extinguished" or annihilated after death. Annihilationism is an attractive belief to many because of the awfulness of the idea of people spending eternity in hell. While there are some passages that seem to support annihilationism, a comprehensive look at what the Bible says about the destiny of the wicked reveals that punishment in hell is eternal. A belief in annihilationism results from a misunderstanding of the consequences of sin, the justice of God, and/or the nature of hell.

In relation to the nature of hell, annihilationists misunderstand the meaning of the lake of fire. Obviously, if a human being were cast into a lake of burning lava, he or she would be almost instantly consumed; however, the lake of fire is both a physical and spiritual realm. The punishment is not simply of a human body; it is of a human's body, soul, and spirit. A spiritual nature cannot be consumed by physical fire. It seems that the unsaved are resurrected with a body fit for eternity just as the saved are (Revelation 20:13; Acts 24:15). These bodies are prepared for an eternal fate.

Eternity is another point of contention. Annihilationists are correct that the Greek word *aionion*, which is usually translated "eternal," does not by definition mean "eternal." It refers to an "age" or "eon," a specific period of time. In some passages, however, *aionion* is without question used to refer to an eternity. Revelation 20:10 speaks of Satan, the beast, and the false prophet being cast into the lake of fire and being "tormented day and night forever and ever." These three are not "extinguished" by being cast into the lake of fire, but their torment goes on forever. Why would the fate of the unsaved, who are also thrown into the lake of fire, be any different (Revelation 20:14–15)?

One evidence for the eternality of hell is Matthew 25:46: "Then they [the unsaved] will go away to eternal punishment, but the righteous to eternal life." In this verse, the same Greek word is used to refer to the destiny of the wicked and the righteous. If the wicked are only tormented for an "age," then the righteous will only experience life in heaven for an "age." If believers will be in heaven forever, unbelievers will be in hell forever.

Another frequent objection raised by annihilationists to the eternality of hell is that it would be unjust for God to punish people eternally for a finite amount of sin. How could it be fair for God to take a person who lived 70 years in sin, and punish him or her for all eternity? The answer is that our sin bears an infinite consequence because it is committed against an infinitely holy God. When King David committed the sins of adultery and murder, he prayed, "Against you, you only, have I sinned and done what is evil in your sight" (Psalm 51:4). God is an eternal and infinitely glorious being. Our sin, an affront to infinite worth and eternal glory, warrants an infinite and eternal punishment. The consequence is proportional to the value of the thing targeted. What matters is not the length of time we sinned, but the value of the character of the God we sinned against.

More personally, annihilationism puts forward the idea that we could not possibly be happy in heaven if we knew that some of our loved ones were suffering an eternity of torment in hell. Scripture says, however, that we will not have anything to complain about or be saddened by in the eternal state. God will "'will wipe every tear from their eyes. There will be no more death' or mourning or crying or pain, for the old order of things has passed away" (Revelation 21:4). If some of our loved ones are not in heaven, we will be in complete agreement that they do not belong there and that they are condemned by their own refusal to accept Jesus Christ as their Savior (see John 3:18; 14:6). It is hard to understand this, but we will not be saddened by the lack of their presence. Our focus now should not be on how we can enjoy heaven without our loved ones but on how we can point our loved ones to faith in Christ so they will be with us.

Hell is perhaps a primary reason why God sent Jesus Christ to pay the penalty for our sins. Being "extinguished" after death is no fate to dread, but an eternity in hell is. Jesus' death paid our infinite sin debt so we would not have to pay it in hell for eternity (2 Corinthians 5:21). When we place our faith in Him, we are saved, forgiven, cleansed, and promised an eternal home in heaven. But if we reject God's gift of eternal life, we will face the eternal consequences of that decision.

94. What does the Bible say about soul sleep?

"Soul sleep" is a belief that after a person dies his or her soul "sleeps" until the resurrection and final judgment. The concept of soul sleep is not biblical.

It's true that, in some places, the Bible speaks of those who have died as being asleep. Daniel 12:2 describes the resurrection as the time when "multitudes who sleep in the dust of the earth will awake." The New Testament speaks of believers who are "asleep" in Jesus. In 1 Corinthians 15:6, Paul speaks of those who are "still living," in contrast to those who have "fallen asleep" (see also verses 18 and 20). Luke relates the death of Stephen with the words, "He fell asleep" (Acts 7:60), much the same as how Jesus describes Lazarus in John 11:11 and Jairus's daughter in Luke 8:52. So, for those who expect a resurrection, sleep is a metaphor for death.

Death is a "sleep" for the believer because it is temporary; the resurrection is the "awakening." But what exactly is it that sleeps, and what is awakened? It is the body, not the soul. A body, when dead, appears to be resting in sleep, and that gives rise to the metaphorical usage of *sleep*. But the soul does not sleep. The moment we experience physical death, our souls are transferred to a different place. For believers, to be absent from the body is to be present with the Lord (2 Corinthians 5:6–8; Philippians 1:23). For unbelievers, death means everlasting punishment in hell (Luke 16:22–23).

Until the final resurrection, there is a temporary heaven—paradise (Luke 23:43; 2 Corinthians 12:4)—and a temporary hell—Hades (Revelation 1:18; 20:13–14). According to Jesus' account in Luke 16:19–31, neither in paradise nor in Hades are people sleeping. The three individuals in Jesus' story—Lazarus, Abraham, and the rich man—are quite conscious and active in the afterlife, prior to the resurrection.

Moses and Elijah were not "sleeping" when they appeared with Jesus on the mount of transfiguration. Far from it. They were "talking with Jesus" (Matthew 17:3). Luke gives some additional detail, relating the subject of their conversation: "They spoke about his departure, which he was about to bring to fulfillment at Jerusalem" (Luke 9:31).

In Revelation 6, John sees "the souls of those who had been slain" in heaven (verse 9). These souls are not sleeping; rather, they are crying out "in a loud voice, 'How long, Sovereign Lord, holy and true, until you judge the inhabitants of the earth and avenge our blood?'" (verse 10). They are given white robes and "told to wait a little longer" (verse 11). Nothing in this heavenly scene hints at a state of unconsciousness, oblivion, or sleep prior to the resurrection. The souls in heaven are wide awake.

Still, it can be said that a person's body is "sleeping" while his soul is in paradise or Hades. And that is just how the Bible pictures it. At the resurrection, the body is "awakened" and transformed into the everlasting body a person will possess forever, whether in heaven or hell. The redeemed, made righteous by the blood of Christ, will inhabit the new heaven and new earth (Revelation 21:1). The unredeemed, who remain in their sin, will be thrown into the lake of fire (Revelation 20:11–15).

Present-day advocates of the doctrine of soul sleep include Seventh-day Adventists, Jehovah's Witnesses, Christadelphians, and some others.

95. What does the Bible say about purgatory?

In short, the Bible says nothing about purgatory. But, since many people believe in purgatory, regardless of the Bible's total lack of information about it, we should discuss the doctrine.

According to the *Catholic Encyclopedia*, purgatory is "a place or condition of temporal punishment for those who, departing this life in God's grace, are not entirely free from venial faults, or have not fully paid the satisfaction due to their transgressions."[21] In other words, in Catholic theology purgatory is the place where a Christian's soul goes after death to be cleansed of the sins that had not been fully paid for during life. Is the doctrine of purgatory in agreement with the Bible? Absolutely not!

An idea foundational to the doctrine of purgatory is that some of a believer's sin has not yet been paid for. But Scripture teaches that Jesus died to pay the penalty for *all* our sins (Colossians 2:13). The Suffering Servant of Isaiah 53:5 took our place: "But he was pierced for our transgressions, he was crushed for our iniquities; the punishment that brought us peace was on him, and by his wounds we are healed." Jesus suffered for our sins so that we could be delivered from suffering. To say that we must also suffer for our sins is to say that Jesus' suffering was insufficient in some way. To say that we ourselves must atone for our sins is to deny the adequacy of the atoning sacrifice of Jesus (1 John 2:2). The idea that those who are saved by grace through faith have to pay for their sins after death is contrary to everything the Bible says about salvation.

The primary scriptural passage Catholics point to for evidence of purgatory is 1 Corinthians 3. Verses 10–15 picture the Christian life as a building project, with the caution that "each one should build with care" (verse 10). Our work will be tested and "will be shown for what it is, because the Day will bring it to light. It will be revealed with fire, and the fire will test the quality of each person's work" (verse 13). At the judgment seat of Christ, we must give an account of what we've done for Christ. First Corinthians 3:14–15 then says, "If what has been built survives, the builder will receive a reward. If it is burned up, the builder will suffer loss but yet will be saved—even though only as one escaping through the flames."

According to 1 Corinthians 3, if our works are of good quality ("gold, silver, costly stones," verse 12), they will pass through the "fire" unharmed, and we will be rewarded for them. If our works are of poor quality ("wood, hay or straw," verse 12), they will be consumed by the "fire," and there will be no reward. The fire is not literal in this passage, any more than the "gold" is literal gold or the "hay" is literal hay. The passage does not say that *believers* pass through the fire but that a believer's *works* pass through the fire. That is, the works are put to the test. First Corinthians 3:15 refers to the believer "escaping through the flames," not being cleansed by the flames. There is no *purging of sin* here, only a *testing of works*.

Purgatory, like many other Catholic dogmas, misrepresents the nature of Christ's sacrifice. Catholics view the Mass/Holy Eucharist as a re-presentation of Christ's sacrifice, ignoring the fact that Jesus' once-for-all sacrifice was absolutely and perfectly sufficient (Hebrews 7:27). Catholics view meritorious works as contributing to one's salvation rather than recognize that Jesus' payment has no need of an additional "contribution" from us (Ephesians 2:8–9). Similarly, purgatory is taught to be a place of cleansing in preparation for heaven, overlooking the truth that, because of Jesus' sacrifice, we are already cleansed. We are also justified, forgiven, redeemed, reconciled, adopted, and sanctified.

The very idea of purgatory and the doctrines that are often attached to it (prayers for the dead, indulgences, meritorious works on behalf of the dead, etc.) implies that Jesus' death was insufficient to pay the penalty for sin. The Bible says that Jesus, who is God incarnate (John 1:1, 14), paid an infinite price for our sin by providing the only acceptable sacrifice (1 John 2:2). To limit Jesus' sacrifice to atoning for original sin or sins committed before salvation is an attack on His person and work. If we, in order to be saved, must pay for our own sin, then Jesus' payment was not enough. If ridding ourselves of sin requires us to suffer interminably in purgatory, then Jesus' suffering and death did not provide a powerful, perfect, and sufficient sacrifice.

Due to Christ's death and resurrection, the believer's position in heaven is as secure as can be. It's as if we are already there: "It is by grace you have been saved! And God raised us up with Christ and seated us with Him in the heavenly realms in Christ Jesus" (Ephesians 2:5–6 BSB).

After death believers are "away from the body and at home with the Lord" (2 Corinthians 5:8; cf. Philippians 1:23). Notice that this verse does not say, "Away from the body and in purgatory suffering in cleansing fire." Because of the powerful, perfect, and sufficient sacrifice of Jesus, we are taken immediately into the Lord's presence when we die. Because we are in Christ, we are fully cleansed, free from sin, glorified, and perfected.

96. What does the Bible say about reincarnation?

To reincarnate is, literally, to "incarnate again"; that is, reincarnation is a "rebirth" into a new body of flesh and blood. In most contexts, *reincarnation* refers to the process, after death, of a soul returning in a new body. Claims of remembering a "past life" imply reincarnation.

According to some religious and philosophical systems, reincarnation involves more than human souls and bodies: a dog's spirit can reincarnate as another dog, for example, or a human soul can reincarnate as a cow. Reincarnation, also referred to as the transmigration of the soul, rests on concepts such as the eternal, uncreated nature of the soul and the need for the soul to "mature," grow, transform, and evolve.

Of course, there is no "proof" for reincarnation. Any evidence put forward is entirely subjective: feelings of déjà vu, recurring dreams, feeling one has an "old soul," irrational phobias, and an affinity for other cultures and eras are all interpreted, by some, as confirmation that they are living another life in a different body.

The concept of reincarnation, in any of its forms, is completely without foundation in the Bible. The truth is that we die once and then face judgment (Hebrews 9:27). The Bible never even remotely suggests that people have a second chance at life or that they can come back as different people or animals. Reincarnation has been a popular belief for thousands of years, but it has never been accepted by Christians or followers of Judaism because it is contradictory to Scripture.

Several passages in Scripture refute the idea of reincarnation. Jesus told the criminal on the cross, "Today you will be with me in paradise" (Luke 23:43)—not "You will have another chance to live a life on earth." Matthew 25:46 tells us that, upon death, believers go on to eternal life while unbelievers go on to eternal punishment. We are created as individuals, and our identity does not change after death (see Luke 9:30).

Some who believe in reincarnation point to Matthew 17:10–13 as biblical support for reincarnation. The disciples ask Jesus about the commonly taught prophecy that Elijah must come before the Messiah (verse 10; cf. Malachi 4:5), and Jesus responds by identifying the "Elijah" of the prophecy as John the Baptist (Matthew 17:11–13). However, Jesus was not teaching that John the Baptist was Elijah reincarnated. For one thing, Elijah did not die; he was taken to heaven in a chariot of fire (2 Kings 2:11), so the literal "coming" of Elijah would have been a descent from heaven, not a reincarnation. Jesus calls John the Baptist "Elijah" because he came "in the spirit and power of Elijah" (Luke 1:17), not because he was Elijah in a literal sense. Also, Elijah himself had just appeared, talking with Jesus (Matthew 17:3), which shows that Elijah had not changed his identity—he had not become John. Finally, the people had earlier asked John the Baptist if he was Elijah, and he said, "I am not" (John 1:21).

Belief in reincarnation is a central tenet in most Indian religious traditions such as Hinduism, Sikhism, and Jainism. Many modern pagans also believe in reincarnation, as do some in the New Age movement, along with followers of Spiritualism. For the Christian, however, there can be no doubt: Reincarnation is unbiblical and must be rejected as false.

97. If reincarnation is not true, why do some people remember their past lives?

Reincarnation can be defined as "the idea that human personality (or a component of it) may survive after death and later become associated with another physical body; as a rebirth of the soul, self or spirit."[22]

The Bible never addresses reincarnation specifically, but it doesn't need to use that term to refute the idea behind it. The biblical model of life, death, and afterlife is incompatible with any form of reincarnation as posited by religions such as Hinduism, Buddhism, and certain New Age or neo-pagan belief systems. Hebrews 9:27 puts the whole notion of reincarnation to rest: "It is appointed for man to die once, and after that comes judgment" (ESV). This single verse eliminates the possibility of reincarnation. Whatever people are "remembering," it is not a past life.

Another verse that counters the notion of reincarnation is Luke 23:43. As Jesus hangs on the cross, He tells the repentant thief next to Him, "Truly I tell you, today you will be with me in paradise." The implication is that, if the man will be with Christ in paradise that very day, he will not be reincarnated back into an earthly life. Similarly, passages such as James 4:14, which addresses the temporal nature of human life, are inconsistent with the idea of living earthly lives over and over for centuries, millennia, or all eternity.

Further, the Bible records instances of people seeing the spirits of long-dead people. Moses and Elijah, for example, were seen by some of the disciples in Matthew 17:3 during the transfiguration of Christ. Such an encounter would be impossible if reincarnation were true.

But how are we to answer those who claim they have memories of past lives? Some have recounted details of life in a bygone era and seem to have vivid memories of people, places, and events that they claim to have experienced. Many reports have been from children and have been the subject of various studies. Do these reports prove that reincarnation is a valid experience?

The first question we should ask is whether these "memories" are genuine. Human memory is notoriously unreliable (just ask any lawyer or detective), and people frequently misremember things. A person can be "sure" of something that never actually happened; another can totally forget things that did happen. Are those claiming to remember a past life misremembering images from TV shows or movies? Are they imagining they experienced events from books they read years earlier? Are they honestly mistaking dreams for genuine memories? What about fraud? In the case of children, could their "memories" of a past life be suggested to them somehow by relatives familiar with the family history or by other things they have seen and heard?

The fact is there is no solid evidence that memories of past lives are genuine. The human imagination is a powerful thing, as is the tendency toward embellishment. At the same time, human memory is a faulty thing. Ultimately, the question comes down to what is the source of truth. Is truth to be found in the unreliable minds of fallen and fallible human beings or in the timeless, holy Word of God? Christians can confidently assert that reincarnation is not a possibility for the human soul. When this life ends, our eternity in the afterlife begins.

98. What does the Bible say about near-death experiences?

A near-death experience (NDE) is an incident in which a person who is at the brink of death is revived and, upon recovery, reports a spiritual experience during the time he or she was unconscious and near death. The memories are often vivid and involve an out-of-body experience, a meeting with dead family members, seeing a white light, or some sort of vision of heaven or hell. There is no specific scriptural support for near-death experiences.

Some people use 2 Corinthians 12:2–4 as a biblical proof text for near-death experiences. In that passage, Paul writes,

> I know a man in Christ who fourteen years ago was caught up to the third heaven. Whether it was in the body or out of the body I do

not know—God knows. And I know that this man—whether in the body or apart from the body I do not know, but God knows—was caught up to paradise and heard inexpressible things, things that no one is permitted to tell.

However, applying Paul's experience to the modern concept of an NDE is taking liberty with the passage. There's nothing in the text to say that Paul was near death (or actually dead) when he found himself in heaven. Paul is simply relating a vision that God gave him of heaven. Assuming this was a near-death experience goes beyond what the Scripture says.

That being said, it is not impossible for God to give someone near death a vision of heaven. If God wants to relate some information to a person suffering trauma, that's His prerogative. If He chooses to allow a nearly dead person to see some relatives in heaven, He certainly can do that. However, with the completion of the biblical canon, we should not expect visions to be normative for Christians. Also, when Paul returned from his journey to paradise, he was silent about what he heard: "No one is permitted to tell" of those things, he said (2 Corinthians 12:4). Has God changed His rule today, and now people *are* permitted to tell?

We need to be extremely careful how we validate our experiences. The most important test of any experience is comparing it with the Bible. Satan is always ready to deceive and twist people's thinking. "Satan himself masquerades as an angel of light" (2 Corinthians 11:14). The unchanging Word of God must take precedence over anyone's experiences, no matter how "real" they seem.

It would be too strong to state that all near-death experiences are faked, imagined, or satanic, but there are still serious concerns, biblically, about their validity. Again, any description of a near-death experience should be held up against the truth of Scripture. If such an experience comes from God, it will line up with what He has already revealed in His Word and ultimately bring Him glory in the name of Jesus Christ.

99. Is the idea of seven heavens / the seventh heaven biblical?

People sometimes use the idiom *seventh heaven* to refer to an experience of great joy, ecstasy, or pleasurable contentment. The expression itself implies that there are seven heavens or seven levels of heaven, a teaching found in several non-Christian religions.

Two very old religions teach the existence of seven heavens: Hinduism and the ancient Babylonian cult. In Hinduism, there are seven higher worlds and seven lower worlds; the earth is the lowest of the higher worlds. The six higher worlds above us are places of increasing wonder and delight where people who have accumulated good karma go after they die. The seventh heaven is, of course, the best. When the dead have spent all the time their good deeds have earned them, they are reincarnated and return to earth. Those who live extraordinarily pious lives can break out of this cycle and experience nirvana, a state of eternal existence.

The ancient Babylonians did not teach that the seven heavens were for humans; rather, they divided the heavens into seven levels of space between the earth's atmosphere and the spirit of the heavens. Beyond was the zodiac. Each of the seven heavens was associated with a particular god and a celestial body: the moon, Mercury, Venus, Mars, the sun, Jupiter, and Saturn.

Historians aren't sure when the Jews first learned of Babylon's seven heavens; Abraham might have been exposed to such a belief before he left Ur, or Hebrew scholars may have learned of it while exiled in Babylon. Either way, rabbis adapted the myth, integrating it into the Talmud—their extra-scriptural writings. The Jewish "heavens," associated with the various celestial bodies, contain a mix of people, angels, demons, Nephilim, and natural phenomena. The specifics of the myth changed with the teacher. As the astronomical and meteorological sciences have advanced, Jews have rejected the idea of a literal seven heavens and now see them as metaphorical—there's no way hail could come to earth from Jupiter, after all.

Islam combines the seven heavens of Judaism with a story from Zoroastrianism. Hadith literature tells how Muhammad was taken on a journey through all seven heavens. In each heaven he met a character from the Bible or another prophet of Islam. Centuries prior to Muhammad, the Zoroastrian priest Arta Viraf supposedly made a similar trip to heaven. In both Islam and Zoroastrianism, the seven heavens are levels of paradise reserved for increasingly devout worshipers.

The Italian poet Dante Alighieri combined Babylonian mythology with Christian metaphor when he wrote *The Divine Comedy*. In Dante's epic poem, the seven celestial bodies represent ever more virtuous natures. Above these heavens, in which the righteous are rewarded after death, are four more levels. The last is empyrean, the true paradise and immaterial dwelling place of God.

The Bible says nothing that would validate a belief in seven heavens, but the word *heaven* itself can have several meanings. The Hebrew for "heaven," *shamayim*, only appears in the plural form and can mean "sky" (Genesis 1:8–9), "outer space" (Genesis 22:17), or "the place where God dwells" (Joshua 2:11). In the New Testament, the Greek *ouranos* can mean "the dwelling place of God" (Matthew 12:50) or "the sky" (Acts 10:11). And *paradeisos* ("paradise" or "garden") can refer to the place where dead believers await resurrection (Luke 23:43), to where God dwells now (2 Corinthians 12:4), or to our eternal home (Revelation 2:7).

In 2 Corinthians 12:2 Paul says he knew a man (assumed to be himself, although he is speaking in the third person) who was taken to "the third heaven." The "third heaven" here simply refers to the spiritual dwelling place of God, as opposed to the other two "heavens"—the atmosphere and outer space. The three "heavens" implied in 2 Corinthians 12:2 would be the three different realms that we call "the sky," "space," and the "spiritual heaven."

In our vernacular, *seventh heaven* means "the best, happiest place to be," but the Bible doesn't give any indication that a seventh heaven actually exists. God promises He will not always live above us, but He will live with us in the New Jerusalem (Revelation 21). And although we will receive rewards according to our works (Revelation 22:12), the Bible never suggests that we'll be segregated into various levels of heaven.

100. What is the biblical view of mortality?

Mortality is the state of being subject to death. Since Adam and Eve's sin in the Garden of Eden, all earthly life became subject to death (Genesis 2:16–17; Romans 5:12). Now, "people are destined to die once, and after that to face judgment" (Hebrews 9:27). The biblical view of mortality is that it is an inevitable part of the curse. The death that comes is the wages of sin (Romans 6:23), but death is not the end of our existence.

All mortals die, and death ends the earthly phase of existence. But according to Scripture, when our bodies die, our spirits are instantly transferred to another place. There are only two possible destinations for our souls after we die physically: heaven and hell. Jesus' story in Luke 16:19–31 plainly shows the difference between those destinations. Those who know Jesus Christ as Lord and Savior are, upon death, immediately in a place of comfort and rest in the presence of God until the resurrection of their bodies (2 Corinthians 5:8; 1 Corinthians 15:16–21). Those who rejected Christ's sacrifice for sin or trusted in something other than the grace of God to save them (Ephesians 2:8–9) will, upon death, enter a place of torment commonly called hell. At the final judgment, all who died in their sin will be cast forever into the lake of fire (Revelation 21:8; Matthew 25:41).

The Christian is aware of his or her mortality and is at peace with it. Death is not to be feared. Physical death merely ushers us into the presence of Christ (Philippians 1:23; Luke 23:43). We should live in a state of prepared expectancy, investing our lives in that which is eternal (Matthew 6:19–20). We will give an account for what we did with what we were given (2 Corinthians 5:10). God wants to reward His faithful servants who invested their time, passions, and resources in His work (Matthew 5:12; Luke 6:23, 35; 1 Corinthians 3:14; 9:18). For the Christian, physical mortality merely results in a change of address, as we move from the tent to the place of permanence (see 2 Peter 1:13–14).

For unbelievers, however, mortality opens the doorway to the worst part of their lives. Those who reject, ignore, or substitute something else for Christ have already lived their "best lives now." Regardless of how miserable their earthly lives may have been, they face greater suffering when the righteous judgment of God falls upon unrepentant sinners (Mark 9:44–49; Revelation 14:10–11; Matthew 25:46). According to the Bible, there are no second chances after death. No purgatory. No possibility that those still on earth can "pray them into heaven."

Some people are terrified to consider their own mortality, but ignoring it won't make it less of a reality. Wise people consider their own mortality and adjust their lives so that they are prepared for it. "The prudent see danger and take refuge" (Proverbs 22:3). We don't know how many days God has appointed for us (Psalm 90:12; 139:16). No one is guaranteed a long earthly life, nor are we guaranteed more opportunities to repent before we die (Hebrews 12:17). The biblical view of mortality is that all human beings will die physically, but only those who are not in Christ will also die spiritually.

Notes

1. G. B. Hardy, *Countdown: A Time to Choose* (Moody, 1971), 31.

2. Albert Barnes, *New Testament Notes: Explanatory and Practical*, ed. by Robert Frew (Baker Book House: 1983), Vol. 1, "Jn. 9:41," 285.

3. Johnny Cash, "No Earthly Good," from *The Rambler*, Columbia Records, 1977, www.johnnycash.com/track/no-earthly-good-6.

4. J. I. Packer, *Growing in Christ* (Crossway, 2022), 187–8.

5. Albert Barnes, *New Testament Notes: Explanatory and Practical*, ed. by Robert Frew (Baker Book House: 1950), Revelation

6. R. Jamieson, A. R. Fausset, and D. Brown, *A Commentary, Critical, Practical, and Explanatory on the Old and New Testaments* (Revell, 1871), 644.

7. Benjamin Franklin, *Poor Richard's Almanack*, June 1746.

8. *Strong's Exhaustive Concordance*, Blue Letter Bible, www.blueletterbible .org/lexicon/g3857/kjv/tr/0-1.

9. Randy Alcorn, *Heaven* (Tyndale: 2004), 319.

10. Augustine, *City of God*, Book XXII, ch. 17.

11. John Piper, "Matrimony No More," Desiring God, October 9, 2017, accessed October 30, 2024, www.desiringgod.org/articles/matrimony-no-more.

12. *Seder Nashim, Kiddushin* 72b.

13. R. Albert Mohler, Jr., "Doing Away with Hell? Part One," Albert Mohler, March 8, 2011, https://albertmohler.com/2011/03/08/doing-away-with-hell-part -one.

14. Dr. Thomas Nagel, *The Last Word* (Oxford University Press: 1997), 130.

15. Louis Berkhof, *Systematic Theology* (GLH Publishing, 1938), chapter V, section A.2.

16. Alistair Begg, "Is Hell an Actual Place?" Christianity.com, YouTube video, December 27, 2017, https://youtu.be/ycrg9Q8x8dc, accessed November 17, 2024.

17. Arthur W. Pink, *The Redeemer's Return* (Bible Truth Depot, 1918), ch. 8, pt. 5, 291.

18. L. S. Chafer, *Systematic Theology*, Vol. IV: Ecclesiology––Eschatology (Dallas Seminary Press, 1948), 406.

19. Catholic Catechism, part 2, sect. 2, chap. 1, 1.vii, ¶ 1281 (United States Catholic Conference, Inc., 1997).

20. Mishnah Eduyot 2:9, Shabbat 33a.

21. Catholic Answers, "Purgatory," accessed May 28, 2025, www.catholic.com /encyclopedia/purgatory.

22. Lucam Moraes, et. al., "Children Who Claim Previous Life Memories: A Case Report and Literature Review," *EXPLORE* 20, no. 6 (2024), https://doi.org /10.1016/j.explore.2024.103063.

Acknowledgments

A special thanks goes out to Kevin Stone and Athalia Bufano, who spent countless hours compiling, editing, and proofreading the answers that went into this book. I'd also like to thank the staff of Got Questions Ministries. Without their hard work, commitment, and passion, this ministry would not be possible. So, thank you to MeLissa Houdmann, Elizabeth DeVore, Kevin Stone, Gwen Sellers, Dianna Merrell, Jeff Laird, Robin Bower, Tiffany Shelton, Athalia Bufano, Nelson Domingues, Emanuel Rodriguez, and Joel Burris. Thank you, also, to the more than eight hundred individuals who have served as volunteer question answerers for GotQuestions.org in the past twenty-two years. GotQuestions.org never has been, and will never be, a one-man show. Above all, to God be the glory—great things He has done (Romans 11:36)!

Shea Michael Houdmann is the president, CEO, and founder of Got Questions Ministries, the parent organization of GotQuestions.org, one of the most frequently visited Christian websites in the world, with over 2.5 billion pageviews in twenty-three years. With GotQuestions.org having received over one million questions submitted from people around the world, Shea has tremendous insights into the questions people are actually asking. He has earned a master of arts in Christian theology from Calvary Theological Seminary and a master of theology with an emphasis in apologetics from Dallas Theological Seminary. He is also currently pursuing a doctor of ministry degree from Dallas Theological Seminary. Shea and his wife, MeLissa, have been married for twenty-eight years. In his limited free time, Shea loves dating his wife, watching and playing sports, hiking, off-roading, movies, and hanging out with his German Shepherd.

NOTES

NOTES

NOTES

NOTES

NOTES

NOTES

NOTES